Waterfowling

Waterfowling

BEYOND THE BASICS

M. D. JOHNSON

PHOTOGRAPHY BY JULIA C. JOHNSON

STACKPOLE
BOOKS

Published by
STACKPOLE BOOKS
5067 Ritter Road
Mechanicsburg, PA 17055
www.stackpolebooks.com

Printed in China

First edition

10 9 8 7 6 5 4 3 2 1

Photographs by Julia C. Johnson, except where otherwise noted

Library of Congress Cataloging-in-Publication Data

Johnson, M. D.
    Waterfowling : beyond the basics / M. D. Johnson ;
photography by Julia C. Johnson. — 1st ed.
        p.   cm.
    Includes index.
    ISBN-13: 978-0-8117-0205-8
    ISBN-10: 0-8117-0205-7
    1. Waterfowl shooting—Anecdotes. I. Title.

SK331.J64   2008
799.2'44—dc22
                                        2007019313

For Julie, just because.

And to the Unusual Suspects—
you know damn well who you are. . . . Thanks, men.

Contents

Acknowledgments ix

Foreword xi

Introduction xiii

CHAPTER 1   Divers Down! 1

CHAPTER 2   A Sea Duck Primer 16

CHAPTER 3   Layout Hunting: Walking on Water 30

CHAPTER 4   Small Duck Skiffs 42

CHAPTER 5   The Care and Feeding of Duck and Goose Calls 54

CHAPTER 6   Mysteries of the Blind Bag 64

CHAPTER 7   Cyber-Scouting and Today's Waterfowler 76

CHAPTER 8   Thirty-One Hardcore Waterfowl Strategies 82

CHAPTER 9   ABCs of Goose Hunting 94

CHAPTER 10   Rails and Snipe: A Marshland Tradition 104

CHAPTER 11   Snow Removal 118

CHAPTER 12   Back to (Shooting) School 130

CHAPTER 13   The Goose Gurus 142

CHAPTER 14   Specialized Spreads for Canadas 152

CHAPTER 15   Today's Hunter: The Modern PR Specialist 162

Manufacturers' Listing 171

Index 173

Acknowledgments

As WAS THE CASE WITH OUR FIRST TWO
waterfowl books, this project is the result
of a collective effort. True, I've been blessed
to have seen and done quite a bit in thirty-three years;
however, I haven't seen it all. And I'm coming to the
realization that I just might not see it all. That's all
right, though, because as you read down through the
list below—a virtual *Who's Who of Waterfowling*—you'll
begin to see that this isn't *my* book, and these aren't *my*
thirty-three years of waterfowling experience rehashed
for your reading enjoyment. No, sir. It's ten years here,
forty years there. It's saltwater, freshwater, big geese,
little geese, boats, skiffs, dogs . . . it's everything, and
it's timeless. Look below, will ya? There's fifty decades
or more of *I've seen that, I've done that, I've been there,*
and perhaps most significantly, *Let me tell you about it.*

Whose book, then, is it? Story, perhaps, is a better
word, and these, good people, are the storytellers:

Bill Cooksey: Four-time Tennessee State duck
calling champion. Can't say thanks enough for all
the opportunities. Tell Little Bill we said hey.

Tim Grounds, Fred Zink, Scott Threinen, Bill
Saunders, Shawn Stahl, Field Hudnall, Kelley Powers:
Championship goose callers, all, and men we're proud
to call friends. Thanks for your time and your patience.

Buck Gardner, Barnie Calef, Rod Haydel: Championship duck callers, and again, good friends. Your help
over the course of the past decade has been invaluable.
A mere thank-you seems insignificant, but thank you.

Tony Vandemore, Tyson Keller, Chad Belding,
Travis Mueller, Curt Wilson, Paul Beyer, Tony Toye,

Richie McKnight, George Lynch, Allan Stanley,
Christian Curtis, Mike & Dan Minchk, Alex Langbell, Randy Bartz, Clay Hudnall, Doug Hess: These
men epitomize the very core of today's waterfowler.
It has been our honor to share blinds, boats, and pits
with the likes of these gentlemen.

Mark Rongers and The Mighty Layout Boys: We
were told, prior to meeting Rongers, that he was of the
"finest caliber." Our source was correct. Everyone should
have a Mark Rongers in his or her life at least once.

Phil Bourjaily: Shooting Editor for *Field &
Stream* magazine and a green-wing teal fanatic after
my own heart.

Steve Sutton: Duck boat enthusiast, decoy carver,
and consummate waterfowler. *With the heady smell
of marsh grass ricocheting through my olfactory . . .* yeah,
whatever. Couldn't have done it without you and your
supreme guidance. Thanks for the harlequins, surf
scoters, and Jack.

Photographers Tony Vandemore, Tyson Keller,
Doug Steinke, Travis Mueller, Alex Langbell, Curt
Wilson, and other members of the Avery Pro-Staff
Team: From Julie and me, thank you so very much
for your incredible visual contributions to this project.
I'm sincere when I say we couldn't have done it with-
out you and your talents behind the digital equipment.
And to those I might have forgotten, my humblest
apologies, please.

A special note of thanks to Joe Fladeland of Bis-
marck, North Dakota, for his wonderful photography.
Just seventeen years old, Fladeland, a member of the

The art that is waterfowling is as traditional as these hand-carved canvasback decoys and the Mississippi River on which they rest.

Avery Outdoors Youth Field Staff, *is* the modern waterfowl hunter, a remembrance of days when every young man had an old pump gun, a self-trained hound, and a true and lasting love for the whole of the Great Outdoors. From Julie and myself—thank you, not only for your digital contributions, but for renewing our faith in the tradition that is hunting.

Mick & Sue Johnson: My folks. These books and my experiences are a result of your teachings, your time, and your unconditional love. Thank you so very much.

Mary Schram & Gordon Walling: Julie's mom and dad, and some right special and very wonderful folks.

Margaret, Jet, and Deacon: A special thanks—and a swat on the ass—to the Dogs of Terror.

Foreword

PERHAPS IT'S THE SOLITUDE. YOU REST AT anchor, often in heavy seas. Three-foot chop isn't uncommon. Dressed for the weather, you lie stone still. All around you, nature's in chaos. Leaden skies move swiftly overhead; you scan the horizon. Wind-driven spray buffets the canvas shield behind you.

In front, the decoys dance on their tethers, throbbing on the long lines that secure them to the lake floor. Prone, you rest eye to eye with your imposters. Shore? 'Tis many miles away. Your mates in the tender boat keep a watchful eye, but for now, you are alone. It is at this moment that I, the waterfowler, am most alive.

Something in the distance tears me from my thoughts—a disturbance in the meeting of water and sky. Then, over the waves, again. A knot of ducks, most likely bluebills, flies as though searching for something. Something only the ducks know. Onward they come. For now, it's eyes and ears—hopeful that the scene will play out as I've imagined.

Two hundred yards downwind and quartering, they act as one. Forty, perhaps fifty 'bills have spotted the stool. Muscled wings propel chunky bodies forward. My heart rate increases; I dare not move. At one time distracted, I now lie focused. Pinpoint precision. They've closed to within 30 yards and, webbed feet splayed, the mass prepares to settle.

Mark Rongers—friend, and co-creator of The Mighty Layout Boys.

Season after season, this scene repeats itself. Spring and summer bring joyful moments with family and friends; later, we work diligently on the decoys, rigging and repainting. Still, the heart of the layout hunter is always, at least partially, suspended inches off the bottom of a small boat—at water level—tethered far offshore on the broadwater.

During 2006, I had the distinct pleasure of meeting M. D. and Julie Johnson, and sharing time with them on the mighty Mississippi River. Though not miles offshore, we were still aware of our surroundings. And our safety.

A word about Julie. I am deeply moved by this consummate sportsperson. She not only knows her way around a marsh, lake, or woodlot, but can call turkeys with the best of them. She is also the most adventurous salmon and trout chaser I've met. Years spent camping in her native Pacific Northwest while in search of both fish and game have made Julie an expert. And expert, too, is her photography.

M. D., by my estimation, is at home anywhere. His presence is one of intense study and "in the moment" awareness; his experience belies his youthful appearance.

And as his writing proves, he is one of our most important contemporary outdoor journalists. What an honor it was to share time on the broadwater with them.

Here in *Waterfowling: Beyond the Basics,* you'll find many things. My passion—layout hunting—is but one. For those unfamiliar, layout hunting was conceived after the ban on sinkboxes went into effect during the early part of the twentieth century. 'Fowlers wanted a way to return to where the birds wanted to be and yet remain within the law, thus prompting the layout boat's original concept and design. This style of hunting will likely never be practiced on a large scale; still, there are those who will always strive for something different. They are drawn to the wonder and awe of fowl that congregate far offshore and—theoretically—well out of harm's way. They love being eye-to-eye with birds in flight, seeing every feather detail on a mature drake redhead at 60 feet. The feeling of isolation while immersed in the grand scheme of nature is addictive.

It's all addictive.

Mark Rongers
The Mighty Layout Boys
Hobart, Indiana, 2007

Introduction

I HAVE A CONFESSION TO MAKE. ORIGINALLY this work was to be titled *Advanced Waterfowling.* Or something like that—something dealing with advanced. As such, I felt a need to define this word, advanced, and that's precisely where the problems began.

You see, waterfowlers have a difficult, if not impossible time agreeing on much of anything. The best shotgun. The perfect shot size. The ultimate decoy spread for divers. Or mallards. Or Canadas. It really doesn't matter. Opinions in the waterfowling world are—well, short of the crude cliché, everyone's got one or two. Or twenty. But I digress. . . .

As I started putting this, my wife and mine's sixth full-length work, together, I asked my waterfowling brothers-in-arms their thoughts on this word, advanced. And it quickly became apparent that this was going to be no different in terms of agreement. You see, one man spoke fondly of diamond-plate jet sleds powered by the latest technological achievements in High Performance Turbo-Hyperdrive Propulsion Systems. Okay, so I'm making that one up, but it's not too far removed from the truth, trust me. His goal, he explained, was to get to those places accessible only to the ducks themselves—that was, until now. That, he said, was his idea of advanced.

Next, I asked a young man, mid-20s, for his thoughts on the matter. "I want to learn to call geese," he said without hesitation. "Not just make the sounds, but really

Tony Vandemore's Ruff stands at the ready during Missouri's spring conservation season. PHOTO BY AVERY PRO-STAFF

call. I want to know what they're saying. I want to be able to communicate." A modern-day Doctor Dolittle, aspires this young man. And it makes sense. Education is advancement.

Then, as is oft the case, I'm thrown for a loop. A veteran waterfowler, a gentleman of the Pacific Northwest with a reputation for knowledge and expertise far beyond his years afield, tells me, and quite matter-of-factly, that advanced to him is a small wooden duck skiff, a spread of hand-carved and painted decoys, and a 50-year-old side-by-side. Traditional, yes. Admirable, certainly. But advanced? It's very possible, I gathered

This scene from Iowa truly defines the craft that is modern waterfowling.

from our all-too-brief conversation, to progress—to advance—while at the same time taking, by popular definition, multitudinous steps backward.

So I sat, as is oft the case, accompanied by three fingers of Gentleman Jack, and pondered my most impromptu research. Futuristic, I discovered, is advanced. So, too, is improving one's abilities in present-time. But, lest we forget, so too are methods of old. All radically different, and yet all—somehow—advanced.

Armed, now, with this conflicting information—this plethora of definitions for but a single word—what'd I do? Simple: It's my book. I changed the title. Why? You want to know the truth? Well, sir, here's the truth, according to M. D. Johnson. Advanced, as it applies to waterfowling, has no definition. It's the ultimate, my friend, in gray area. That man with the $15,000 duck boat? The one with the heated-kitchen, 150-horsepower jet pump, and cable-ready TV? Ready? He may not be a waterfowler. Oh, he may kill a duck or wayward goose here and there, but consis-

tency? He may not have it. He's got the gear, all right, but he just might lack the know-how. The street smarts. The been there, done that. Money can't buy experience. Only time buys experience.

Now, you see that bedraggled looking bloke unloading the 10-foot pine wood—yep, that's home-spun camouflage, all right—pirogue out of the back of that old Ford? Well, sir . . . he's going to take that blade and paddle himself out underneath those ducks that have been trading back and forth. Once he's out there, he'll throw out six, maybe eight very realistic, hand-carved decoys. Then he'll lie on his back, cover up, stay hidden, not move, and not feel obligated to put his lips around that piece of plastic hanging around his neck *every* time he sees a duck. And when the time comes, he'll kill what he's shooting at. When he's done, he'll pick up and go home. He'll kiss his wife, hug the kids, pluck his ducks, take out the garbage, drink a Blue Ribbon, and go to bed. To me? That's advanced.

Advanced, as I see it, is all about consistency . . . and that's a word you'll see often in the next 150-some odd pages. But it's also about innovation. It's about adaptation and improvisation. It's all about trying something different, breaking away from the norm, having it fail, and then having the—let's call it testicular fortitude—to try something just a little bit different. Advanced? That's probably not the best word

To me, the pursuit of diving ducks on the Columbia River is advanced. Why? It's personally uncharted territory to a great extent.

choice here. Maybe innovative. Or unique. Perhaps . . . beyond the basics?

So here are the bottom lines (and you thought I'd have but one?) and then we'll move on. Advanced doesn't necessarily mean more birds on the ground. A $15,000 skiff doesn't define the phrase advanced duck boat, no more than the waterfowler afoot spells backwards. The ON/OFF switch on a spinner won't make a damn bit of difference if you can't hit your butt with both hands at the same time when it comes to shooting that fowling piece—accuracy trauma shows no favoritism. Advanced, and here's the key, is in the eye of the beholder. To the man in the Columbia River estuary, advanced is a wooden scull boat and a flock of undisturbed widgeon. For Mike Minchk on the Mississippi, it's a two-man layout that he shares with his son, Dan, and the ability to say, "I learned this myself." To the man with the deep pockets, it's diamond-plate, hyper-drives, and all the electric gadgetry known to the Lord above . . . and then some. For Washington's Steve Sutton, it's gunning over a spread of hand-carved and painted decoys, while for Shawn Stahl of Michigan, advanced is the perfection of his art—the art of two-way conversation with Canada geese. To each of you reading this, advanced means something slightly different. That's great. That's fine. In fact, that's the reason behind this book. It's like Red Green—the next best thing to come out of Canada since Shania Twain and Mike Myers—says: "I'm pullin' for ya. We're all in this together."

And we are.

M. D. and Julie Johnson
& The Dogs of Terror
June 2007

CHAPTER 1

Divers Down!

GIVE ME A MINUTE, LET ME THINK, AND I should be able to tell you about my first diver. Or rather, my first diver encounter. You see, I was raised as a puddle duck man by a puddle duck man. Mallards, blacks, woodies, bluewings—we had 'em all in the northeast Ohio beaver swamps where I spent my formative waterfowl years, a period also known as the 1970s. But divers? Ah, we knew about them. We heard the stories about guys killing redheads and canvasbacks and bluebills on the great bays of Maumee and Sandusky, but our personal experience was limited to just that—stories.

It was 1987, perhaps 1988. I was living in Columbus at the time, and spending every duck season weekend on the Scioto River near the small town of Circleville just a short drive south of the capital. I remember it was bitterly cold; in fact, a few days after my father, Mick, killed what was to be our first diver—a hen American (common) goldeneye—I went to the local clinic where my tingling fingertips and peeling, grey skin told of frostbite. But I was twenty-four then, young and invincible, and the inconvenience of a tender trigger finger was just that, an inconvenience.

The goldeneye, as I identified her to my non-diver father, was unintentional; a bonus bird that simply passed by, on her way elsewhere, our spread of oversized Carry-lite mallards. It was a start, nonetheless—an ember in my brain. Smoldering, yes, but alive.

Works of art—handcrafted canvasback decoys owned by Mark Rongers of The Mighty Layout Boys.

Washington, October 1993, and I had added five unique species of waterfowl to my personal hunting journal, including ringnecks—or as they're called in the Pacific Northwest, ring-bills—bufflehead, scaup, and a lone drake hooded merganser that was destined for a place of honor on the wall. Like my father's first non-dabbler, divers were to me still a case of happenstance. New to the eye and to the hand, and incredibly quick on the wing, these unusual birds presented a formidable challenge to one schooled on lumbering mallards, black ducks, and Canada geese. Somewhere, deep in the recesses, the ember was beginning to take on a life of its own.

It was with a young man by the name of Tony Toye, a seasoned guide working the historical waters of the

Mississippi River not far from his home in southern Wisconsin, that in November 2000 I hunted divers specifically. Not just any diver, mind you, but the King—the canvasback. Then thirty-six, I remember grinning like a 14-year-old holding hands with the new girl when the autoloader bucked and the slope-nosed drake tumbled into Toye's set of magnum blocks. Excited? Hell, I wouldn't even let our guide's three-legged chocolate lab, Deacon, get him. No, sir; that bird was mine. And while Toye shook my hand, and my wife Julie gave me a hug, the ember that had sparked that frigid December morning on a little river in central Ohio started to blaze.

Three years later. I'm reclining on a secluded sandy spit of land that juts out toward a channel marker on the Columbia, my neoprene-clad length concealed in a tawny, lightly grassed layout blind. Jet, my wife's 8-year-old female black lab, lies next to me. Twenty-five yards out from where the waters lap at the shore, sixty decoys bob in the slight chop. They're all black and white decoys—four mainlines of leaded crab cord, each weighted with a 10-pound vinyl-coated mushroom anchor and finished with a two-pound grapple at the tail. Fifteen drake bluebills are tethered to each run, all with a 36-inch dropper (too short, and the dog gets tangled between runs) and a 5-inch stainless steel halibut clip. The three closest lines are run parallel, just enough clearance between them to easily paddle an AquaPod through. The fourth, or outermost line, begins at the tail third of the last parallel string and curves out toward the mainstem of the river like a black-and-white velvet rope at a movie theater.

When the first small knot of 'bills appears downstream, flying low over the water, I reach to my chest, grab a single-reed, and growl at them. Jet's ears perk up and her body tightens; she's seen them now. Closer they come. In unison, left wingtips drop, and the group changes direction, boring in as if on a collision course with the outside run of decoys. Another course change, this time to the right, and a dozen webbed feet drop. Jet rises slightly, and I start to slide the autoloader to my shoulder.

Okay . . . I'm better now.

Jet and me on the Columbia River in Washington State doing the diver thing.

Drakes of canvasback, redhead, ringneck, and American widgeon—
as handsome a duck strap as you'll ever find.

My blood brother, Tony Miller—a diehard puddler maniac who periodically will switch to divers.

INCREASED DIVER POPULARITY

Why, seemingly all of a sudden, my interest in divers? For that matter, why are waterfowlers across the country turning their sights—literally—on members of the diving clan? Mind you, not everyone's switching from shovelers to scaup or baldpate to bluebills. No, sir; there are plenty of diehard, wouldn't have it any other way, puddle duck fans out there. Still, it's tough to argue this rise in popularity.

There are probably several explanations for this change. And while I'm not a biologist nor psychologist, I'll take a stab at the possible reasons behind the shift from dabblers to divers.

Age and Opportunity

Let's face it . . . waterfowlers in this country are, as a group, getting older. I read recently that the average hunter in the U.S. is 46 years old. Chances are as you read this, that number has gone up to 48, or maybe even 50. Regardless, we duck and goose hunters are graying—or, if you're anything like me, graying *and* getting a bit rotund 'round the middle.

As hunters age, we go through what's known as the five stages. These include the following.

Stage 1: The hunter bases the success or failure of an outing on the number of shooting opportunities presented; that is, a lot of shooting means a good hunt, and vice versa.

Stage 2: Here, the quality of the hunt is based on the number of animals harvested. A limit of ducks constitutes a good hunt; two or three birds, a fair outing.

Stage 3: In stage 3, it becomes a hunter's goal to harvest a certain type of game—a drake canvasback, a Eurasian widgeon, or a banded Canada goose, for instance. A unique experience is a quality experience.

Stage 4: Our hunter is a bit older, or rather, more experienced. And as such, he enters stage 4, where he exhibits a desire to hunt in a certain, perhaps unique manner. He takes up layout hunting. He carves his own decoys or builds his own duck boat. Or, just maybe, he switches from mallards to mergansers. This is Method Man.

Stage 5: Recreation, pure and simple. He's harvested enough game so as to satisfy his bloodlust. He has a unique specimen or two on the wall or the photo album, and he can look back and say about any number of different hunting techniques, "I've done that." Don't get me wrong; this man's still a predator, and a good one. But he's often just as happy being out-of-doors.

Note: Not every hunter goes through all five stages. Some folks, in fact, will get stuck in, say, one of the first two and never, well, evolve. You might also have a stage 5 man who's 30, and another who's 60; everyone's different. Still, these are the stages.

I mention the stages as they relate to divers, diver hunting, and transformed diver men specifically for stages 3 and 4. Personally, this is in large part why I made the switch. I wanted to kill a drake canvasback. I wanted to kill a drake bufflehead, a drake bluebill, and a drake redhead. I wanted to do something different, something I hadn't done before. Layout hunting. Deep water. Gang rigs. Open places. Not that flat on my back in the middle of the Mississippi was any more exciting than watching a flock of sprig work a decoy spread—it just was something different. I think a lot of guys feel the same way.

Reduced Hunting Pressure

While it may not be the case everywhere, diver hunting pressure—human pressure, that is—and puddle duck pressure are two radically different things. Plain and simple, it's first and foremost a matter of logistics. You have to *want* to shoot divers. In the majority of cases, you have to go there, wherever there is, specifically for divers. And while I run the risk here of irritating some folks (won't be the first time), diver hunting is just flat hard. It's hard work, much more so, I think, than hunting puddle ducks. Finally, there's the specific equipment required. Given a half-dozen Canada floaters and twelve standard mallards, a man can kill any number of puddlers, along with Canadas, snows, specks, and what-have-you. Unfortunately, you can't often, if ever, take that same dabbler/honker rig, toss it out, and expect to shoot a limit of cans or bluebills over it . . . even if the anchors *did* reach the bottom!

So it's like this. Given the logistics, the difficulty, and the specific equipment necessary to be a successful diver man—well, most folks opt out. Combine this with the fact that, mistakenly so, quite a few hunters don't consider divers edible, and you have all the trappings of a solitary hunting experience. Not always, as I said, but solitude—translation: a lack of competition—is one of the reasons why I hunt divers.

Diver Scenics

Myself? I dearly love the places that divers call home. Sure, I enjoy going back to the beaver swamps of my native northeast Ohio. Or to the shallow rivers or wide

*Chasing divers often brings decreased hunting pressure—not always,
but often enough for many to give it a good, hard look.*

A knot of scaup, aka bluebills. PHOTO BY JOE FLADELAND

flooded impoundments of the Midwest. The Dakota potholes, too, hold an attraction; still, there's just something about the Mississippi. The Columbia. Saginaw Bay. Maumee. Chesapeake. Something about water I can't wade. About the wind and the waves, and tiny flashing dots of black and white that streak across the rollers as if they could fly right through you. There's that. For the man who's spent his entire life hunkered in a rice levee or crouched in a box under a century-old oak on a riverbank, these are mysterious places. Mysterious, and irresistible.

Disposable Income

Here again, brutal honesty. Hunting is no longer an inexpensive sport; however, as an aging group, hunters, and waterfowlers seemingly in particular, have more disposable income. Thus, whereas twenty years ago many a man couldn't afford the necessary equipment—boat, motor, layout boat, decoys, and so forth—to make the switch from blue-wings to bluebills, today many a

Facing page: I simply love the places that divers live, such as here on the Mississippi River off the Illinois town of Nauvoo.

man can. Certainly not everyone, but more folks than in yesteryear.

MEET THE DIVERS

So there you have it. Truthfully, the reasons a man discovers divers are both many and few. But just who are these feathered devils that cloud men's thoughts and fly as though Old Patch were after them? And are capable of frustrating even the likes of Saint Peter were he a diver man—which he probably is when he isn't watching the gates.

For the diver men, the principle players in the game include the following.

Canvasbacks: If divers were whiskey, the canvasback would be Gentleman Jack, which, at least to me, is as good as you get. True, his numbers are down. Some years, we can have one; others, as it was while I was growing up in the late seventies, he's off limits entirely. Either way, he's wonderful. He's magnificent on the wing, and tremendous on the table. And while I damn near hate to make the comparison, I think it only fair to say the drake canvasback is the 190-inch whitetail of the diver man's world. I know he is in mine.

Above: Winchester's Kevin Howard with a fine Oklahoma pair—redhead and can. *Right:* Gunning a variety of divers on Washington's Columbia River. Though uncommon at this very location, cans are definitely a possibly.

Redheads: I feel almost the same with redheads as I do with cans. There's just something about them—like that breathtakingly pretty girl at the dance, the one that you just couldn't work up the gumption to ask out under that spinning mirrored ball. Close, but unattainable. If you do work up the courage and she says no, you're deflated. On the other hand, if you ask and she says yes—well, that's a limit of drake redheads.

Greater and lesser scaup: Listen to me . . . I love bluebills. They're James Bond stark in their formal attire, with a glare that says—in no uncertain terms—I'm not messing around. And the blue with the black? Incredible. Add the fact that 'bills are kind to the taste buds, more than capable on the wing, typical suckers for a well-located spread, *and* often responsive to imitations of the drakes' grumbling growl, and you've got a winner, wings down.

Bufflehead: Layout fanatic Mike Minchk, whom you'll meet later, refers to buffleheads as the "teal of the diver world" in reference to their magnificence on the table. While I don't doubt Michael, I personally haven't found the proper recipe for 'heads; that is, I'm not much on them. Visually, though, the cocky little drakes can't be beat—purple iridescence, white-on-black contrast, snow goose-pink feet. They are incredibly strong fliers, too.

Ring-necks: Another very "contrast-y," predominantly black and white bird, if there were such a word. Very handsome—maybe that's better. Ring-necks are an interesting half-diver/half-dabbler combo; that is, they look like divers, fly like divers, but can often be found sharing the same shallow water, tip-up habitat with mallards, teal, and the like. To me, ring-necks offer the best of both worlds. I find them very good on the table, and, like many divers, tremendously acrobatic and challenging on the wing. Small freshwater ponds ringed with Douglas firs and alders, just inland from the Pacific so as to mute the crash of the surf—that's where I dearly love hunting ring-necks.

Common and Barrow's goldeneyes: The visual differences between the common and Barrow's goldeneyes are subtle, save for the facial patch worn by the drakes. On the common or American, as he's sometimes known, this swatch of white 'tween bill and eye is round; with the Barrow's, the similarly located patch is a crescent. Both are a formal black/white mix, of medium size, and swift of wing. Whistlers, that's what they're called, and it takes but one near encounter to understand why. (Note: It's the wings.)

Washington diver man Fred Slyfield, who along with his waterfowling fanatic sons, Hunter and Spencer, operates Caribou Creek Outfitters on more than 100 river miles of the Columbia between the town of Brewster and the Tri-Cities Area downstream. "We shoot common goldeneyes," says Slyfield, "and the occasional Barrow's, but we usually have to set up specifically for them. The goldeneyes seem to want to decoy to their own species, and they really seem to have a mindset about what they're doing and where they're going." A little Type A/anal retentive for a duck, but that's goldeneyes.

Mergansers: We had a standing rule about mergansers when I was a Washington resident: "You shoot it;

Right: A small flock of redheads come into a North Dakota pothole. PHOTO BY JOE FLADELAND *Below: Challenging on the wing and delectable on the table, bluebills are as traditional as waterfowl itself.* PHOTO BY JOE FLADELAND

Ringnecks, sometimes call ringbills, are a wonderful little duck—almost a cross between diver and puddler, and excellent on the table. PHOTO BY JOE FLADELAND

you eat it." Funny, but no one I hunted with ever killed one. Now there are guys who shoot them and, I'm assuming, include them in the year's batch of breast fillets destined for the sausage grinder; however, I'm going to take a pass, thanks. Sure, the common/American and the red-breasted merganser are big birds; still, and short of the aforementioned sausage, pepperoni, or truckload of garlic, I find them rather—well—unpalatable. The hooded merganser, a much more handsome bloke, I think, than either of his larger cousins, may be bit more flavorful given his penchant for habitats offering more in the way of edible vegetation.

THE BOATS AND BLINDS

Over the course of my diver education, I've learned that the boats and blinds used to hunt these species are as varied as the birds themselves. Combination boat blinds—a powered hull with a camouflaged blind constructed atop—are the more commonly seen watercraft employed for both getting to the birds *and* hiding from them. Hunters gunning from layout boats—small, no-motor, low-profile skiffs that are essentially water level blinds—will use a second, larger tender boat. It's the motorized tender's responsibility to set the layout, rig and retrieve the decoys, and pick up any fallen birds. On calmer waters, smaller skiffs such as the Carsten's Canvasback or the ultra-traditional Barnegat Bay Sneak Boat are often used.

And finally, there are land-based blinds. On a recent hunt along the Columbia, my blind was the root-ball of a long-dead fir, conveniently washed ashore at the end of a long timbered point; the 'bills, goldeneyes and buffleheads paid me no mind. Another day, I hid myself in a lightweight Avery Power Hunter layout blind on a bare sand spit behind four dozen drake bluebill blocks—that day, my hide and the birds worked wonderfully. The lesson here is—as Clint

A drake common goldeneye, one of several beautiful specimens taken throughout the season by Fred Slyfield of Caribou Creek Outfitters in Washington.

Eastwood said in the movie *Heartbreak Ridge*—improvise, adapt, and adjust.

THE DECOYS

Diver decoy variables—numbers, arrangements, anchors, cords, and so on—are based primarily on two factors: location, and species. The rule of thumb is big water equals big numbers, big decoys, *and* bright colors; smaller waters translate into smaller spreads of perhaps life-size versus magnum decoys.

Big water often presents visibility problems; that is, the birds can, due to elements such as distance or waves, have a difficult time seeing a decoy spread. Big numbers of big (magnum or super-magnum) decoys, then, coupled with the eye-catching white of the drakes of species such as cans and bluebills, help to ensure the rig is seen. On smaller waters, this visibility factor isn't as crucial; thus, smaller numbers, and very natural-looking decoys such as Greenhead Gear's life-size blocks can often work just fine.

Divers are some of the more species-specific waterfowl when it comes to decoys. That's not to say that you won't kill cans over a bluebill spread—it's certainly possible—only that if you want to consistently fool

bluebills, you use 'bill decoys. For cans, it's cans, and so on. Goldeneyes are perhaps the most notorious in terms of their own kind. Whether common or Barrow's doesn't seem to make a difference, only that the blocks are goldeneyes. Buffleheads, too, can be very decoy specific; fortunately, there are ultra-realistic 'eye and bufflehead decoys available.

Today, most diver men, myself included, rig their decoys using what's known as a long-line method. Each decoy is rigged with its own dropper cord—in the case of my divers, a 36-inch strand of heavy tarred cord. A large stainless steel clip called a gang clip is attached to the dropper, and is used to quickly clip each decoy to the mainline. Mainlines and anchors both differ with the user and the situation. My mainlines consist of 90 feet of leaded (sinking) crab line. A brass clip at one end allows me to attach my head or lead weight, an 8-pound mushroom anchor; a second brass clip at the opposite end is used for a 1.5-pound grapple style tail weight. Once in position, I attach the

Washington's Mike Wolski, a recognized waterfowl outfitter, and partner pull longlines with the help of a 17-foot TDB (The Duck Boat).

Top: Here, I'm preparing to drop a 10-pound mushroom anchor to the bottom of the Columbia River. This will serve as my head or lead weight on a multi-decoy mainline. PHOTO BY NICHOLAS MILLER *Above: A 1.5-pound grapple weight serves as a tail (end) anchor on a longline. Sometimes more weight might be necessary.*

head weight and drop it over while backing the boat, by current or motor, down. As I back away from the head weight, I clip individual decoys onto the mainline—usually a dozen or so per line. Then, making sure I have enough line at the end to reach *and* hold the bottom, I'll snap the grapple weight and toss it over. This method allows large numbers of decoys to be set out and picked up quickly.

A couple notes on decoys. *Do* use droppers long enough—I like 36 inches—so that a dog can swim across the lines without getting tangled in the main-

The AquaPod by ATTBAR, Inc.: a small skiff, but an extremely versatile duck boat.

line. I shouldn't have to explain that tides, current, waves, half-inch leaded rope, and heavy anchors can all spell disaster for an entangled retriever.

Do use anchors appropriate for your situation. On the Columbia River, and given the current and tides, I'll use the aforementioned 8-pound and 1.5-pound combination; inland on still waters, I'll often use the 1.5-pound grapples as both head and tail weights.

Do not be afraid to experiment with the decoy riggings; that is, the arrangement or pattern. My favorite bluebill set on the Columbia consists of three parallel twelve-bird lines 8 to 10 feet apart just upwind of the blind, with the outermost line about 30 yards out. In front of the blind, I'll rig a blob of a dozen 'bills on single anchor cords—this represents the mass scramble for an obvious food source. Finally, and at the downwind edge of the blob, I'll run one more twelve-bird line out and away at a 45-degree angle. Traveling birds often follow this angled line into the mass and in front of the guns; the three twelve-bird lines help attract attention.

Above: Wrapping the rig after a successful morning's hunt. To the diver man, decoy and line organization is a must. Right: Kevin Howard with Winchester's newest offering, the Super X3—a fine performer under even brutal weather conditions.

THE GUNS

For divers, I shoot the same Winchester Super X2 (Modified choke) that I shoot for puddle ducks and geese. In terms of ammunition, 3-inch steel #1s or #2s are fine in most situations; high-velocity steel is even better, particularly on windy days. Better yet are some of the non-steel/non-toxics, with my favorites being $1^{1}/_{4}$ ounces of Hevi-Shot #4s. With the exception of buffleheads, most divers are big, strong, well-feathered, and heavily muscled birds; light loads often won't cut it.

THE TABLE

Anyone who doesn't hunt divers because "divers aren't edible" hasn't had them fixed properly. Good friend and Washingtonian, Tony Miller, makes a killer blue-

bill stir-fry. Steve Sutton, another avid 'fowler and Evergreen Stater, did a side-by-side comparison of sautéed surf scoter and goldeneye this past winter, and Julie and I enjoyed both immensely. Mike Minchk, a layout fanatic from eastern Iowa, refers to buffleheads as "the teal of the diver family," and that's saying a hell of a lot for buffleheads. As I've discovered, the keys to good-eating divers are four:

1. Clean them as soon as possible after harvest.
2. Remove *all* the fat.
3. Soak the breasts or birds in salt water overnight.
4. Cook them rare.

Then, don't be afraid to say it, "My name's Mister X, and I'm a diver-holic."

The Flyways' Best Bets

There are places synonymous with diver hunting: traditional waters whose mere mention conjures up vivid images of flights of bluebills winging through wind-driven snow, or small knots of lordly canvasbacks sculling swiftly overtop the whitecaps. These are the historic haunts of the diver men, and of the birds that have come to symbolize the purest essence of waterfowling. There are others, of course, not named here; but these, quite simply, are some of the four flyways' finest.

Atlantic: Chesapeake Bay

Some will disagree, I know, but I'm not sure if there's a more traditional body of water for the diver men than the grand Chesapeake Bay. Like all of the United States, the Bay and her shorelines have and have been changed over the past century; still, the waters of the Chesapeake continue to attract scores of waterfowl throughout the fall of the year, and along with them, the gunners.

Variety is the star of the Chessie's show. Cans, redheads, 'bills, goldeneyes and mergansers share the true diver spotlight; three subspecies of scoter—white-wings, blacks, and surfs—and oldsquaws are available for diver men wanting to make the switch, even temporarily, to the seaducker's lifestyle.

Mississippi: Mississippi River

The Mississippi River and divers go together like Liz Taylor and ex-husbands. I killed my first canvasback on the river in 2000, so the Old Man holds a special place in my waterfowling journal. And as I did, many a duck hunter travels to the Mississippi for an opportunity to harvest a can; however, the river offers a diverse diver menu, including redheads, 'bills, goldeneyes, buffleheads, ruddy ducks, and ringnecks. The Old Man is one hunting area I'd highly recommend.

Central: The Impoundments

I'm awful hard-pressed to pick one best bet when it comes to divers in the Central Flyway, a problem that isn't necessarily a bad one to have when you're an avid diver man. If you're into still water, there are the impoundments—eastern Kansas's John Redmond Reservoir or Calamus Reservoir in north-central Nebraska come immediately to mind. So, too, does North Dakota's Devil's Lake, or as good friend, avid 'fowler, and former Grand Forks resident, Lee Harstad, calls it, "Diver Central."

Pacific: The Columbia River

I'll admit it openly: I'm partial, above all the diver waters in the country, to the Columbia River in Washington State. The Columbia has it all—scenery, shallow water, deep water, islands, sloughs, solitude, and a variety of diver species enough to make a box of 64 Crayola crayons look like just another lead pencil.

The Columbia in central Washington plays host to redheads, canvasbacks, bluebills, buffleheads, goldeneyes, and ringnecks. Downriver and where the Columbia forms the border between Washington and Oregon, the rafts are often made up entirely of scaup, with the occasional bufflehead or goldeneye to keep things interesting. Likewise on the stretch from the Vancouver metropolitan area downstream to the estuary, the gunning is primarily a 'bill show; however, the estuary does offer a greater variety, including the opportunity to tag a wayward white-winged or black scoter.

Anyone who tells you that divers aren't good on the table has never had them prepared properly. PHOTO BY FRED SLYFIELD

CHAPTER 2

A Sea Duck Primer

I F THE ESSENCE OF WATERFOWLING INDEED lies not in the kill, but in the whole of the experience . . . if the sights and the sounds and the touch are to the hunter as gold coins are to the miser, then sea duck hunters are the richest 'fowlers by far. For theirs is an ever-changing world made radically different four times each day by the combined efforts of the moon and Mother Nature. Their schedules are ruled not by the clock, but by the tide's constant ebb and flow.

The pursuit of sea ducks—eiders, oldsquaws, scoters, and that most handsome little clown, the harlequin—isn't, even for the experienced puddle ducker, an "I think I'll do this today" sort of proposal; it's too different from the waterfowling that the vast majority of us grew up with. Certainly, there are exceptions, and these exceptions almost without fail are known as Washington sea duck hunters. Or in New England, sea duck gunners. Or they call the open waters of the Chesapeake Bay home. It's a unique world—a fascinating world, this realm of the sea ducker. The decoys are strange, the lines are long, the weights are heavy, and the water dark and often brutally cold. And the birds . . . they're not your typical mallard or sprig—no, sir.

In recent years, a greater number of diehard puddle duck enthusiasts have turned to sea ducks as a sort of personal challenge; the next step, many will tell you, on their individual journey along hunting's five steps from shootist to tactician. Steve Sutton is one such

Sea ducks, such as this surf scoter (left) and harlequin, are essentially indescribable in their beauty.

*Above: Steve Sutton's "courting" goldeneye decoys lend a air of realism to a sea duck spread. **Left:** Georgia native turned Washingtonian, Steve Sutton—waterfowler, conservationist, birder, and very good friend.*

individual. A native of Georgia, Sutton hunted divers—scaup, ringnecks, the occasional redhead, and the even more occasional canvasback—extensively in his home state and neighboring Florida. It wasn't until 1972 that, while in North Carolina, he hunted sea ducks for the first time. "I was fascinated," he says, "by the major differences in hunting sea ducks and any of the other ducks I'd hunted up until then—the open water, the long lines, the way the sea ducks decoy and fly, and how difficult they are to kill." In the mid-1980s, Sutton moved to Washington State, and since then has hunted sea ducks on both coasts. "Eiders and oldsquaws in Maine," he says. "Scoters in New Jersey, scoters and eiders in Massachusetts. On the West Coast, I've hunted Washington, Oregon, and British Columbia for all of the species we consider sea ducks here."

In January of 2006, my wife, Julie, and I had the opportunity to spend several days on the water with Sutton as part of a fact-finding and photographic venture we were at the time working on. The month prior, I'd had the pleasure of gunning the waters of Maine's

Penobscot Bay for eiders, oldsquaws, and scoters. Sitting down with the information and images we'd gathered, and as a newcomer to the world of sea duck hunting myself, I found it incredibly helpful as part of my passage through the five stages of the hunter, to put together what I refer to as a "Sea Duck Primer"—a unique look into the world of the saltwater-fowler.

EIDERS

Hunting eiders, I quickly discovered, is a challenge from the start. First, and as is the case with any type of successful waterfowling venture, you have to know where the birds are. "You can definitely scout for sea ducks," says Sutton. "They favor different feeding and loafing spots based on tide levels, *but* the problem with scouting sea ducks is that in a lot of cases, the birds might only use the area that you happen to have spotted them for a couple hours of each tide. Remember that the tides are an hour later the following day, and that tidal range—rate of flow—also changes daily. What that means is just because you see birds at a certain spot at

10 A.M. doesn't mean the same combination of factors that caused them to be there will be duplicated the next day. So just seeing sea ducks isn't enough; you have the added challenge of factoring in the other variables as well. Get that figured out, and you should be able to predict when the birds will be in particular areas."

Secondly, either you or your captain has to navigate a craft of sufficient size and seaworthiness over often-long expanses of open, cold, and very deep salt water without careening haphazardly into inanimate objects such as lighthouses, lobster boats, or the huge jutting rockpiles that the Maine folk have taken to calling ledges. Ledges they may technically be; however, to a Midwesterner, there's little difference between a Maine ledge and a good, old-fashioned rock. A big rock.

Then there's the cold—not an ordinary cold that comes and goes, one easily defeated by such things as synthetic fabrics and chemical handwarmers. An East Coast cold, a Maine in December cold, slips through whatever you're wearing and wraps itself around your very soul. An hour into the hunt, and you're more than

A pair of drake common eiders—interesting birds, and some of the most tenacious creatures I've ever encountered.

willing to trade a body part for 30 seconds in a nice, hot shower. But you can't get 'em, the guide will tell you, from the comfort of your brown reclining chair. And he's right. You can't.

And the shooting? Well, slip yourself into 8 to 12 inches of heavy cold-weather clothing, including gloves and a rabbit-lined Siberian musher's hat. Next, balance yourself precariously on, say, five thousand ball bearings, each the size of a 50-cent piece. Periodically, have a friend spray you with ice-cold water. Your task, then, is to place a pattern squarely on something roughly the size of a Nerf football traveling at 40 miles per hour from left to right without straying into the neighboring gun's field of fire. Think it's easy? Plain and simple, it's not.

Finally, there's tenacity . . . and then there are eiders. Densely boned, heavily muscled, and feathered with black-and-white Kevlar, I have in 31 years of waterfowling across the United States never encountered any avian species as difficult to subdue as are eiders. Net one, shake it, and it's not unusual to get a goodly number of your #2 steel pellets back. "If," I heard on more than one occasion during my last trip to Penobscot Bay, "eiders were the size of giant Canadas, I'm not sure you'd ever kill one." Exaggeration? Perhaps, but from what I've seen, it's really not too far from the truth.

"Tight chokes and *big* shot if you're shooting steel," recommends Sutton when talking eiders and gunning. "I shoot 3-inch #2s with steel, and I like a

Gunning eiders off the Maine coast from a 21-foot TDB. Seaworthiness—well, I can't say enough about it out there.

Above: Penobscot Bay Outfitters owner, Todd Jackson, readies a portion of a goldeneye rig during a late morning laid-back diver/black duck hunt. Right: Some of the new exotic (non-steel) waterfowl rounds—Xtended Range, Heavyweight, Hevi-Shot—are the perfect choice for big water gunning and hardcore birds like eiders.

shotshell that moves at least at 1,300 feet-per-second. If I was shooting just eiders—or white-wing scoters—I wouldn't be unhappy with steel BBs. And nothing less than a Modified choke, even if the birds are close. I'd rather miss completely than fringe a bird and have to chase the resulting cripple.

"My rule of thumb: If the bird hits the water with his head up, or if he shows any movement, it should be shot again immediately." Sutton, by the way, speaks highly of Environ-Metal's Hevi-Shot as a non-toxic, yet non-steel alternative for sea ducks. "With Hevi-Shot," he says, "I prefer #4s. I stay with the same modified choke, and find that this combination requires fewer follow-up shots on cripples on the water. For sure, Hevi-Shot is more expensive, but when you look at the cost-per-round versus the total cost of your (hunting) trip, it makes sense—at least to me—to give yourself the best chance."

As for eiders and decoys, it's more where than how or how many. Todd Jackson, owner of Penobscot Bay

Outfitters (888-SEA-DUCK/www.seaduck.net) out of Searsport, Maine, rigs forty full-bodied eiders on a single line—twenty off the bow, and another twenty free-lined at the stern—with his TDB positioned between the blocks. Jackson's partner, Sam Cassidy, likewise splits his decoys evenly on a single mainline with the boat in the middle; however, he uses eighty lobster floats, each painted an eider-like black/white. Twenty floats are pegged with a 1 inch-by-1 inch pine dowel on each of four approximately 100-foot lengths of rope, and each length is stored in its own decoy bag. Once in location, Cassidy drops an anchor line to which is attached the first and second string of floats. A 50-foot dead (no decoys) segment serves as a boat hook-up; then, the third and fourth lines are set followed by a second (tail) anchor. Cassidy's rig is incredibly quick and easy to rig and retrieve, and the fact that the decoys were floats instead of honest-to-goodness plastic eiders seemed to make no difference to the birds whatsoever.

SCOTERS

All three of the world's scoter species make themselves known to sea duck hunters in the United States, with specific populations varying in number depending upon location. "Black scoters are the smallest of the three," said Sutton, "and in my area (Washington) definitely the least common. They're more common in Alaska, but if you wanted to shoot black scoters specifically, the best spots would be the middle Atlantic Coast."

Size-wise, surf scoters fall in the middle between blacks and white-wings, and are, Sutton says, the more numerous. In hand, surfs are a heavy, full-bodied bird, with a massive head, oddly white eye, and equally thick multi-colored bill; this bill, along with the drake's white "cotton patch" on the back of his head, along with a similar patch on his forehead, provide excellent field markings. White-wings are the largest of the three species, only slightly smaller than common

Sutton introduced Julie and me to scoters, as fascinating a species as I've ever hunted.

Above: A scoter rig in progress on coastal Washington waters. Big black decoys mean increased visibility, and it's all about the blocks being seen. Top right: The colors on the drake surf scoter's head need to be seen firsthand in order to be truly appreciated. Bottom right: Yes, Virginia, those are pellet holes. Scoters, like all sea ducks, are tough customers. The key is to shoot—and keep shooting—until it's over.

eiders. Both sexes sport the white speculum (lower wing patch) from which the species draws it name, with the all-black drake showing a white Nike-esque swoosh underneath, like the surf scoter, a white eye.

"All three species will mix together in feeding flocks," said Sutton, "but they prefer to travel in relatively unmixed groups. This isn't a hard and fast rule, though it does seem to hold true where I have hunted them."

Diver hunters should quickly recognize Sutton's typical scoter rig. "Essentially," he says, "I rig for scoters the same way I rig for divers if I'm using long lines. I'll have a long leg, with the last decoy just out of range. In most cases, I'll run that leg across the tide so that birds trading parallel to the tide (flow) can see the decoys better.

"I'll use three or four lines of decoys to form the 'wad' of feeding birds, with a big hole in the middle for the birds to land in," he continues. "It's similar to what you'd do with a diver layout rig, except that with the layout rig, you'd have the blind in the decoys. With the bigger boats commonly used to hunt scoters, you have to 'hide' the boat—you locate the boat off to the side of the rig, not in it. Approaching birds, then, see only decoys, a hole to land in, and open water behind that."

Like eiders, scoters are strong, tenacious birds that require heavier loads of larger steel pellets; similarly, those opting for non-steel/non-toxics may find the increased pattern densities that come with pellet downsizing effective. While hunting scoters with Sutton in January, I shot both Hevi-Shot #4s and Kent Cartridge's IMPACT tungsten-matrix in #5s with excellent results.

OLDSQUAWS

I was raised on teal, and unfortunately I'm familiar with the frustrating aerial antics of these little ducks. That said, I've never seen anything fly like an old-squaw. Give them a little tailwind, and I'm not sure that even high-velocity shotshells can keep up with these swift-winged sea-goers. "Oldsquaws," said Sutton, "are one of the few sea ducks that have the wing loading capability to be able to put on the moves similar to a puddle duck, and they can really be challenging to shoot."

The penchant of the oldsquaw (a.k.a. long-tailed duck) for deeper water presents another challenge. "It's possible to shoot them close to shore," said Sutton, "but in those cases, it will likely be where deep water occurs close to shore. Oldsquaws feed in smaller, looser flocks, and you don't often find them in the same shallow water feeding areas with scoters and goldeneyes."

A self-admitted casual oldsquaw hunter, Sutton sets numerically small rigs when targeting these birds. "The only reason to go with big rigs," he said, "is for visibility, which certainly can help given the open water nature of these birds. Personally, I think you can get that visibility—that lots of white on the water—by using V-boards with silhouettes. [Note: Triangular wooden platforms to which two-dimensional decoys are attached, V-boards elevate decoys off the water, thus increasing the distance from which they can be seen.] That said, there are people who kill a lot more oldsquaws than I do, and they use bigger rigs. If I was going to concentrate on them, I'd most likely go with more decoys."

Interesting to note is the drake oldsquaw's call, an oddly melodic, far-reaching sound commonly referred to as a yodel. "The yodel," said Sutton, "is a contact call. The males do it, and it becomes more common as the season progresses. Since it's a mating call, I believe it can also be used as an attraction. It has to be done by mouth," he continues, "as I know of no call, per se, that comes close to duplicating that sound. I've done it, and would say it's worth the try. If nothing else, you entertain the occupants of the boat."

This "yodeling" oldsquaw decoy sports a tail or sprig carved from caribou bone.

I refer to oldsquaws—or long-tailed ducks, to be politically correct—as sea-going pintails. Right or wrong, it seems to fit.

HARLEQUINS

Raised as I was by a puddle duck man, I spent years in awe of the avian tapestry that is the drake wood duck; that is, until I held my first drake harlequin. Blue, black, white, chestnut—the birds are a blend of beauty and intrigue. Only along the upper West Coast and in Alaska is the hunting of harlequins permitted; an East Coast population exists, though hunting hasn't been allowed since the early 1990s due to numerical concerns.

Today in Sutton's home state, the limit on harlequins is one bird per season. "Washington is unique," he said, "in that we have the only reliable harlequin hunting available in the Lower 48. This one-per-season limit was believed by those who supported the restriction to be the best way to ensure a future in-state harlequin hunting opportunity. Prior to this, population and harvest numbers on Washington harlequins were sketchy at best, and this one-per-season

regulation provides the data needed to be certain that populations aren't being over-harvested, while still allowing those who want to hunt them the opportunity."

Sutton's harlequin rig is, pure and simple, art: thirteen hand-carved decoys representing the work of five extremely talented carvers. These, I was to learn, he rigs close to the cobblestone, shallow water shorelines that harlequins prefer. "Harlequins," he says, "are very shoreline-oriented. They'll loaf in deeper water when the shoreline is disturbed (muddy), but they prefer to be tight to shore. When I rig, I want to be as close to the beach as I can be without the boat grounding out. This ensures my decoys are in the bird's flight path as it trades down the shoreline. And also that they don't fly behind me as they work that shoreline."

Though Washington's waterfowl season begins in mid-October, late November is harlequin time for Sutton. "I typically don't hunt until about Thanksgiv-

You almost don't want to touch them, they're that magnificent. And you sure as hell don't want to put 'em in the water!

Harlequins: The Clown Prince

11 January 2006
The 1,800-mile drive from Iowa to western Washington can now be filed under "the past." It was, as my father is fond of saying, uneventful, save for a short stretch in the Medicine Bow that got hairy. Tomorrow, Julie and I head for the Canadian border with Steve Sutton to try our hand at a first for both of us: harlequins. Odd—31 years since my first duck, and I'm acting like a kid who's been given the key to the candy store. All I know is I gotta go to sleep quick so tomorrow'll come faster.

12 January 2006
Julie and I, skippered by Sutton and joined by his black Lab Mike, launch well after daylight and make our way to the south and west. Sutton's first choice is out. "We'll get beat up by the wind and waves," he tells us. We opt for his second pick. The decoys, hand-carved and painted, represent five artists. Thirteen is all we use; no 100-block spreads for harlequins. They're split about evenly, drakes and hens. We set two lines with four, one with a pair, and three singles. Strange, but one doesn't have a head. Harlequins, Sutton explains, often land and immediately begin feeding—head underwater, searching visually for crabs and other little things. So it's a feeder . . . makes sense. The rig set, we pour coffee and wait. Sutton answers more questions, including "What do harlequins look like on the wing?" The man's incredibly knowledgeable, not only about ducks, but birds in general, and we pass the time talking about what we've seen and what we haven't.

I notice a bird coming from the southwest. I convince myself it's a duck—there are things out here on the salt that I sure as hell never saw in an Ohio beaver swamp. This one's flying like Sutton said a harlequin would . . . then it's gone. Damn boulder! Just about the time I figured it landed, it reappears. "You know," I say, "I think there's one coming." From the stern, Sut-

ing or so. By that time, the drakes are starting to show a lot of interest in the hens, either by following them closely in flight or flying to them when they're alone on the water. I capitalize on this," he explains, "by rigging my decoys to match these habits. Paired birds will land anywhere in the rig, though typically very close to the decoys. Single drakes will in most cases decoy to the single hen." Sutton rigs three decoys—a hen, followed by two drakes—on a single 20-foot line anchored only at one end. Two pairs of

ton, binoculars pressed to his face, confirms: "It's a drake," followed by "and it's an adult." Julie's told to get ready; she looks at me nervously. She hates one-gun pressure, but wraps her hands around the autoloader. The drake, I can see him clearly now, goes to set, and she rises; the bird splashes amongst the trio of singles while the hollow b-o-o-m rebounds off the high bluff behind us. Mike, in classic style, makes a faultless retrieve.

It's funny, but there really was no celebration. More—what should I call it?—reverence, I think. With drake in hand, the hunt continued and yet, simultaneously, was put on hold. I'd grown up, I told

Sutton, with the kaleidoscope that is *Aix sponsa*—the wood duck—but I'd never seen anything like this. Julie held the bird as if it were something breakable—a milkweed pod that at any moment might burst and float away on the winds. I had my chance an hour later, and the hunt once more stopped and the admiration began anew. How could anyone become jaded to something like this?

Julie completes her Sea Duck Authorization (Report) Card, a necessity in Washington State, as Sutton admires the girl's first harlequin.

Above: With Sutton at the helm, I assist with laying out a small harlequin rig on a quiet cove. Left: As fine a pair of drakes—scoter (left), and harlequin—as available, I think, in North America.

lines are placed to the right of the boat, two to the left, with a single hen in the middle of two sets.

Wind, waves, time and tides. These all exist within a world coaxed into life by salt spray, and personalized by the images burned onto the sea ducker's eyes. It's a place, this world, of long, black tails. Of court jester fowl perched atop ages-old stone pedestals, and distant black-and-white eiders that fleetingly mingle with the whitecaps as they ride the netherspace 'tween sea and sky. It's their world, that of the sea ducks, and that of the men who brave the daily rise and fall for just a glimpse, and the grand opportunity to say that they've seen them. A primer? 'Tis true, for it's just the beginning.

*Sutton walks me through my first harlequin set from
anchors and lines to the decoys themselves.*

CHAPTER 3

Layout Hunting: Walking on Water

I'VE HUNTED DUCKS NOW FOR THIRTY-ONE years. And in those three-plus decades, I've had the good fortune to hunt in some fantastic settings with some of the most knowledgeable waterfowlers ever to walk the planet. My wife, Julie, knows this; she's been there for damn near half of those years. So it took us both by surprise when I came home from my first layout hunting experience on the Mississippi River a couple years back, and made the announcement:

"That's it, wife," I said as I walked in the kitchen. "I'm selling what I need to sell, doing what I need to do. I'm buying a 20-foot plate boat and a layout. I can paint all the mallards and widgeon and grey ducks into bluebills and redheads." I was on a roll; there was no stopping the speech now. "I'll have to buy some more cans . . . and I'm gonna start doing this layout diver deal. You should have seen it." And for the next sixty minutes, the poor girl heard it all.

Eventually, I calmed down and decided that my intended selling and painting and buying spree might just have to wait a bit; however, my rethinking it all did little to squelch my fresh-found enthusiasm for this newest of old-time waterfowling methods— gunning ducks from a layout boat.

Pulling the cans from the Mississippi at day's end.

TRADITION EXEMPLIFIED

In the fall of 2004, layout hunting to me was a new venture; that's not to say that layout hunting as an art form is new. In fact, it's anything but. While there were still men crouched in sinkboxes and sculling needle-nosed skiffs burdened with 4-gauge punt guns, 'fowlers lay prone in low-profile wooden craft (the predecessors to today's fiberglass layout skiffs) on waters such as Lake Erie's Maumee and Sandusky bays, Michigan's famed Saginaw Bay, and, lest we forget, those most traditional currents of the Mississippi River. Back then, these gunners surrounded themselves with dozens of hand-carved and painted art pieces, and watched, even then in awe, as great flights of redheads, canvasbacks, bluebills, and goldeneyes swooped from the heavens to light among their counterfeit brethren.

Today, both the sinkboxes and huge punt guns are gone, outlawed as a result of their deadly effectiveness and their potential to forever impact migratory waterfowl populations. Layout boats, however, and the strategies that are their use have survived, and while there are indeed differences now in the twenty-first century—synthetic boats, plastic decoys, and non-toxic shot, to name but three—the tradition that is layout hunting lives on across the United States.

THE MIGHTY LAYOUT BOYS

The Mighty Layout Boys. The name is synonymous with everything that is layout hunting. Cork decoys, boats, longlines, more boats—the boys have it all.

Mark Rongers is one of the boys; one-third of what's become known as the MLB. In 1975, Rongers, along with MLB co-founder, Greg Bires, bought their first layout boats. Secreted in their newly purchased Sneakbox Wigeons, Rongers and Bires learned the tricks of the trade gunning bluebills, redheads, cans, and other divers over a spread of L.L. Bean cork decoys on the waters of southwest Michigan. A year later, the pair were joined by Tom Reder, and the Mighty Layout Boys were officially off and floating.

I don't care how many years you've hunted waterfowl; a sight like this is going to make you catch your breath. PHOTO BY JOE FLADELAND

*Diver men and decoys just go hand-in-hand. This is part of a 125-piece,
all hand-carved rig we gunned over on the Mississippi.*

I caught up with Rongers one summer evening at his home in northwest Indiana, and spent the better part of a hour picking this waterfowling guru's brain.

MDJ: Your first layout hunt was thirty years ago, and you're still very much in love with the sport. What is it that holds you to this style of waterfowling?

Rongers: There's something intrinsically primitive, sometime primeval, about bobbing around, say, two miles from shore on Lake Michigan in a 10-foot or a 12-foot-long boat. You're very much alive when the wind's kicking out of the north throwing two and three-footers, and there's a scudding grey sky in mid-November. When you see that first flock of 'bills on the horizon, something just grips you. You begin to realize your own insignificance in the grand scheme of things. Ultimately, you flashback to being a hunter. I just can't find that excitement, that adrenaline rush, in any other form of waterfowling.

MDJ: Why are men now making the change from non-layout gunning to using layout boats? Why are people becoming layout hunters?

Rongers: What I get a lot from folks who call us is this: "I'm getting tired of sitting on the shore or in a boat blind, and watching birds congregate out in the middle of the lake or in the middle of the bay. I'm tired of doing all this work," they'll say, "and getting very little for it." They'll ask us if layout hunting is the way to go then, and that gets the conversation started. That's a big part of it. And to a lesser extent, I'll get the guy who calls and say he's simply looking for something new.

MDJ: Layout boats are synonymous with diver hunting, but is there a place for layout boats in the puddle ducker's arsenal?

Rongers: Absolutely. . . .

Rongers is, without question, the most humble manufacturer I've had the pleasure of working with on a literary project, and continually stopped far short of praising or, Heaven forbid, promoting his own product, as good as it may be; however, there's a strong point to be made here concerning the use of layout boat in both a diver and a puddler application. That said, I'll paraphrase his response to the last question:

Above: Rongers claims that flagging divers—he's waving the cloth here on the Mississippi—works about one-third of the time. Pretty good odds for anything hunting. Left: Julie hunkered down in a two-man MLB skiff. We didn't have grays, a traditional clothing color choice for layout gunners.

According to Rongers, the switch from the layout as a diver-specific rig to one with puddler possibilities has recent origins in southeastern Missouri. Frustrated by scores of dabblers congregating on large, open-water expanses of flooded agricultural ground, an enterprising group of 'fowlers began building layout-esque boats, skiffs that could be either paddled or motored into position. These were then camouflaged with a combi-nation of cloth and native grasses. Low profile and practically invisible, even to puddlers hovering above on approach, these Four Rivers Layout Boats (www.four riverslayoutboats.com) were the answers to the now no longer frustrated hunters' prayers.

Dabbler men themselves during their formative years and now self-proclaimed opportunists, the guys at MLB recognized the potential of a combination puddler/diver layout rig, and went to work in their own shop. "With the help of a company that does tubing work," says Rongers, "we've created an aircraft aluminum frame that's spring-loaded and hinged to the boat overtop the cockpit. This has a camouflaged see-thru mesh Cordura nylon cover, with loops for adding grass and native vegetation. And I think we're onto something here. As quickly as you put the blind on the boat, three to five minutes later, it's off and you're diver hunting again."

I find it impossible to close this puddler/diver segment without relating a story Rongers told me pertaining to the effectiveness of these traditional layout boats when they're used in a dabbler application:

"My builder," Rongers begins, his grin evident even through the telephone lines, "was in a white Boston Whaler tending to a layout boat that a buddy of his had set in some lily pads on a very heavily-hunted lake here in northern Indiana. Well, during one hunt, he got flagged down by a conservation officer (CO). She directed him over to a boat ramp, and when he motored across, she said 'I want to check your shotgun shells.' And he said, 'Well, okay, but why?' So she told him, 'I see where you're anchored, and I see where those birds are falling. You're a good 100 to 125 yards away, and I want to see what you're shooting at them.' He laughed and said, 'I'm sorry, but there's a layout boat in those lilies over there. That's who's shooting

Right: For me, part of the attraction of layout hunting is the decoys. Here, Julie pulls one of Rongers's artwork canvasbacks. Below: Divers, such as these 'bills, never approach a layout rig at under anything less than what could only be described as blazing speed. PHOTO BY JOE FLADELAND

Big Mike Minchk—former exclusive greenhead gunner turned dedicated diver man. Funny how those things happen.

those birds, not me. I'm just tending to that layout boat.' Then he called our buddy, Jeremy, on the radio, and it looked just like he sat up out of the weeds. The CO was rather embarrassed. But I guess if it tricks COs, it does the same sort of thing to the ducks."

DETAILS, AND A DAY ON THE MISSISSIPPI

Few places in the country are as synonymous with diver hunting as is the Old Man, the mighty Mississippi River. And as such, the Mississippi has for decades attracted the layout men with their small pumpkinseed boats, high-walled tenders, and scores upon scores of cork bluebills, cans, and redheads.

Mike Minchk is one of these men. A wide-shouldered fellow, visually seeming more at home on the gridiron than in his role as a respiratory therapist at the University of Iowa hospital, Minchk, now 46, moved to Iowa City when he was 18; even then, though, he was no stranger to the world of waterfowling. "I grew up hunting around Prairie du Chien with Dad and Grandpa," said Minchk. "We squirrel hunted

as kids," he told me, "and we hunted geese around Horicon Marsh." With his moving to eastern Iowa, he soon began rubbing elbows with some of the finest duck callers to ever come out of the Midwest, mallard maestros the likes of Wendell Carlson and now three-time World Duck Calling champ, Barnie Calef. Eventually, he began calling competitively himself. But, and despite the camaraderie of the contest circuit, there was something missing with the hunting itself. "You had to get out there at midnight to claim your spot," Minchk recalls. "It got to be frustrating."

Having gotten young Dan tucked away in the two-man, father Mike (standing)
and diver partner, Mike Shepard, turn the tender toward shore.

Searching for something new, Minchk and his now 13-year-old son, Dan, began spending time along the Mississippi near the town of Fort Madison in southeastern Iowa. Earlier in his waterfowling career, Minchk had gunned puddlers and divers alike from permanent box blinds situated on the river here. "My wife's from Fort Madison," he told me. "There's still family down there. And we had some truly memorable hunts over the years." But with he and his son's return to the river during the 2000 season, he took with him something new—a layout boat. "The first one," he said, "was a one-man MLB Classic. Four years ago, though, we went to the two-man version."

"It's quite a learning curve, this layout deal," said Minchk. "We read everything we could on layout hunting. And the Internet, too. There's quite a bit of material available there. But it's (layout hunting) all a continual learning process."

The Minchk Boys rigging the spread at first light on the Mississippi.

And so in November of 2004, and again in 2005, thanks to Minchk, Dan, and their fanatical layout hunting partner, Mike Shepard, I got to experience this layout learning curve firsthand. The principle things I learned about layout hunting were two: First, a waterfowler may decide to become a layout hunter overnight, but he doesn't actually become one overnight. And second, successful layout hunting and the phrase "lots of stuff" are one and the same.

Before we touch on the type of stuff, let's first take an elemental look at how layout hunting works. The layout boat itself is transported by the larger, motor-

within effective shotgun range of the layout boat. With a shooter inside the layout, the remaining hunters then pull away, anchoring the tender from 200 to 500 yards distant, where they watch the proceedings through binoculars. Once a bird or birds are downed, the tender unclips from an anchored buoy, retrieves the birds, and returns to the moorage—or switches out, with a tenderman becoming a shooter and vice versa. From what I've seen, it truly is an orchestrated process, with all parties working together in synchronicity.

That said, what does one need to layout hunt? First, there's the tender boat. Minchk currently runs a 25-foot Clark with high sides, a 200-horsepower Evinrude, and side console steering. "My first tender," he said, "was smaller, with a tiller outboard. I liked the maneuverability of the tiller, but in the back, you were always getting wet. The console took some getting used to last year, but I like the mobility." Rongers, too, runs a long tender—a 20-foot runabout—but prefers a Deep-V hull design for the ride. "It's the ugliest boat you'll ever see," he told me over the phone. As for transporting the layout boat to the actual hunting spot, Rongers uses a combination hoist and hydraulic jack system to get his skiff into and out of the water; Minchk, on the other hand, manhandles his two-man over the hull.

Decoys, lines, and anchors come next. "Normally," said Minchk, "we'll carry a hundred burlaped Herters bluebills when we gun the Mississippi."

"Buffleheads, too," Dan quickly adds. "Then there's fifty G&H super-magnum bluebills and fifty G&H super-mag cans." His longlines—100-foot runs of what looked to be half-inch cord—were armed with heavy clips at either end, and were stored on blaze orange electrical cord reels. To set a line, a lead window (sash) weight was clipped to one end and thrown overboard. With the tender in reverse and working up-current, decoys, each with a separate dropper cord and 6-inch stainless steel clip, were snapped onto the mainline. With 20 feet or so to go, the last decoy is clipped in place, and a homemade mushroom style anchor attached. "This rig," said Minchk, "was part of that learning process. You can use a window weight as a tail-weight but not as a head-weight (the up-current weight). The round window weights roll on the bottom, particularly on a sand bottom. They just won't hold."

ized tender boat—usually carried, but sometimes pulled behind—from the launch point to the actual hunting location. Depending on variables such as wind direction, sun, and current, the layout boat is anchored fore and aft in Position X. Using the tender, the gunners then set multiple strings of decoys; each line works to funnel birds from downwind to a point

Bluebills! PHOTO BY JOE FLADELAND

Flat on your back surrounded by little more than water, waves, and cork—that's the layout gunner's lifestyle, and most wouldn't trade it for the world.

Lying at the waterline in the middle of the Mississippi River is an experience
I'll never forget—and one I'll enjoy again soon.

On my hunt, I watched Mike and Dan drop the layout boat and set the lines, helping where I could, and staying out of their way when I needed to. "You're up," said Minchk, swinging the big Clark alongside the anchored two-man MLB, and helping me get myself and my gear inside. Aboard, I quickly discovered two things: First, there's enough room to hold a barn dance inside a two-man MLB layout boat, which is good because at 6-foot, 4-inches, I need all the legroom I can get. And second, the boats are incredibly stable, a nice bit of information seeing as I'd already drained one Thermos of coffee and was starting on my second when they put me adrift.

By noon, and under a high blue windless sky, we were done. Inside Minchk's tender, a trio of drake buffleheads, a redhead, and a pair of 'bills lay as our combined take for the day. "It was slow," my host said as we retrieved the last of the lines. "But it's hard to beat the river for variety," he continued, adding that over the course of a season, he and Dan will typically harvest ring-necks, buffleheads, redheads, cans, greater and lesser scaup, mergansers, goldeneyes, and a smattering of puddle ducks.

"And don't forget snow geese," Dan reminded his father, referring to the lone white goose the boy killed from the layout a couple years back. Motoring back through the rafts of coots, I couldn't help but smile. It's not often that I get to lie flat on my back in the middle of one of the most recognized waterways on the planet and indulge myself as I did that morning. From the bow, Minchk turned, and a grin crossed his face. He'd seen it before—the look—and though I couldn't hear him over the roar of the Clark's 200 horses, there was no doubting what he'd said: "Convert."

CHAPTER 4

Small Duck Skiffs

THE SCENE: WESTERN WASHINGTON. Good friend and waterfowling accomplice, Tony Miller, and I, along with my wife, Julia, and Tony's son, Nick, launch a flotilla of small fiberglass duck skiffs—known both technically and locally as Aquapods—into the shallows of a freshwater pond within earshot of the surf that pounds the coastline. Under cover of a quickly fading night, we paddle and jockey for position as we make our way toward the southern, and hopefully duck-filled, end of the boggy marsh.

Ten minutes of upper body exercise later, a trip punctuated periodically by Miller's cries of "Row, ye scoundrels!" and his son's, "Remind me to drown him, eh?" we're in place. Julie and Nick drape the 'pods with tules, while Miller and I set a mixed spread of divers on the right and puddlers on left. A couple backward glances to make sure everything looks as it should, and we, too, hide ourselves away. The widgeon, green-wings, ringnecks, and bluebills never knew what hit 'em.

A year later and 1,800 miles to the east, colleague in outdoor journalism, Phil Bourjaily, and I are sharing the confines of a 14-foot Carstens Canvasback as we await the morning flights on a large wildlife management area in eastern Iowa. Powered by one of the all-the-rage shallow water outdrive motors, this one a 6-horse Fisher Beavertail, the loaded-down Canvasback glided through 6-inch depths, smartweed, and

A solitary 'fowler paddles his skiff to the east. It's going to be a good day. PHOTO BY AVERY PRO-STAFF

surface clutter like—well, I'm not going to use the knife-and-butter cliché, but you get my drift, right? Picking a spot out and away from the crowds, we tossed out eighteen mallards downwind, eighteen bluebills upwind, and a half-dozen Canada floaters near the boat. Folding chairs were set, my modified scissor blind was raised, coffee cups were filled, and we were ready. From 50 yards away, Bourjaily and I were just another muskrat-constructed clump of stuff. "It's all about low profile out here," commented Bourjaily, taking a swig from his steaming cup. "You know—I could get used to this getting on the water at 8:30 kind of stuff." That day, we shot as the other boats watched.

Behind me, my hosts for the morning, Mike Minchk, and his young but waterfowl-savvy son, Dan,

Left: Picking up a diver rig with a 10-foot Aquapod. On calm waters, we'll often use the 'Pod as tender and layout blind both. PHOTO BY NICHOLAS MILLER *Below: ATTBAR, Inc.'s Aquapod. I've owned four since 1995, and don't have a single complaint about the little boats.* PHOTO BY NICHOLAS MILLER

Clint Robey and his canine assistant pull a lightweight skiff into the cattails after setting a teal rig in central Missouri.

both smiled as they shoved the two-man MLB (Mighty Layout Boys) layout boat over the gunnel of the 20-foot LOWE tender and into the waters of the Mississippi River. Pre-predawn, I'd met the guys not far from their home in Iowa City, and on the drive, listened intently to their tales of in-your-face bluebills, redheads, cans, and other ducks. New to the traditional style of water-fowling known as layout hunting, I was anxious both to photograph the event, and—can't lie to you!—step into the gunner's seat and try my hand.

The boys had been telling the truth. Not long after getting the layout boat positioned and several lines of diver blocks set, I found myself flat on my back in the MLB. Mike and Dan, coffee and hot chocolate steaming and made-fresh in the boat breakfast burritos filling the void, sat in the big LOWE some 200 yards away, watching through binoculars. Everything was ready.

I'd love to say my first attempt at gunning from a rocking layout boat went well; it didn't. Nor did my second or third tries; however, when the fourth small

knot of 'bills screamed into the decoys, I somehow managed to splash a black-and-white drake into the lines. Behind me, I heard the big 200-horse burst into life, and seconds later, Minchk was handing me my first open-water diver. "Had enough," he asked, hand-ing me my drake and a burrito. At his side, young Dan was grinning the "I've seen that look before!" smile.

"You know," I mumbled, bits of egg and onion collecting in my beard, "I think I'll stay here for a while longer, if that's all right."

Quick! List me an element common to all three stories, aside from the fact that each deals with water-fowling and the unfortunate reality that is my poor shooting? And the survey says: small boats—one or two-hunter skiffs, if you will, that serve a specialized purpose above and beyond simply getting gunners out to a hunting location, and then perhaps serving as a water-top blind. In the first tale, we find 8- and 10-foot muscle-powered watercraft. The second highlights an almost 15-foot skiff propelled by a shallow-drive motor

and topped with a customized and heavily camouflaged blind, all while maintaining the low profile necessary to be effective. Finally, there's the layout blind—an unpowered hole in the water that fills the bill as a blind, yet requires the use of a larger boat, the tender, in order that the hunters be successful. All boats, all small, all different . . . all sneakboats?

Before we go any farther, let's stop and get everyone on the proverbial same page as far as the phrase sneakboat is concerned. In a generic sense, the term sneakboat can be used to define a small, say 14-foot and under, water-going vessel employed in the hunting of waterfowl. This boat may be powered by an internal-combustion engine, an electric motor, paddle, or oars, or occasionally, Mother Nature. When in use, this skiff may either be anchored as in the case of a traditional layout boat, stationary as with a camouflaged marsh boat, or as with a scull boat, constantly in motion. True sneakboats, it appears, may either be staked in place or, as was traditional, drifted into rafts or small flocks of ducks; however, I'm getting ahead of myself.

Left: *This 14-foot Carstens Canvasback allows me to haul larger-than-normal spreads into the field should I deem such an undertaking necessary—which I usually do.*
Above: *Tony Miller uses a 10-foot Aquapod to set a diver rig on the calm waters of a Columbia River estuary.*

To help explain the differences among the vessels within this admittedly generic category known as sneakboats, let's look at each separately; however, I do want to preface these definitions with a disclaimer of sorts. In the waterfowler's world, a layout boat is a layout boat, and a scull boat is a scull boat. These particular skiffs won't be used interchangeably, no more than a hammer will replace a screwdriver or vice versa. That said, one man's sneakboat might be another man's marsh boat—or again, vice versa. Definitions can differ, as do uses, options, means of power, camou-

flage, and other variables, so please keep this in mind before you disagree.

Sneakboats

An excellent example of a traditional sneakboat, I think all will agree, is the classic Barnegat Bay sneakboat. Such sneakers are characterized by longer hulls (12 to 14 feet) and extremely low profiles. Today the phrase sneakboat has gotten away somewhat from its original meaning and is being used to describe any small one to two-man duck boat, regardless of how that boat is used.

Why put it away in December? We use our Carstens Canvasback year-round.

Traditionally, sneakboats were used as such. A large decoy spread was set, and the sneaker anchored some distance away upwind or up-current—say, 200 yards. Once a goodly number of birds were sitting in the blocks, the boat, with the gunner lying low, was unclipped and allowed to drift down into the unsuspecting birds. From here, it became a lot like layout hunting, with the shooter sitting upright and taking birds as they flushed.

Today, however, this style of hunting, though still practiced by a handful, is practically unheard of. Instead, these modern sneakboats—Barnegats, the Carstens Canvasbacks, for example—are often fitted with a blind, equipped with a small outboard or shallow-drive motor, and used as a both a conveyance and a hiding place, thus transforming them, some say, from a true sneakboat to more of a marsh-style skiff. It's all in the eye of the beholder, methinks.

Marsh Boats

As mentioned, there may or may not be a whole lot of difference between the sneakboats and the marsh boats of the twenty-first century. If there were, it might be that marsh boats—the Aquapods, Stealths, Fat Boys, and Puddlers, to name but a few—are a bit smaller in length than the sneakers, averaging from 8 to 12 or 13 feet, and are typically powered by upper body strength. Again, and this all said, I have used my 14-foot, 4-inch Canvasback, with an internal-combustion motor, as a marsh boat. Likewise, I know of several folks who power their skiffs with two- or three-horse outboards or high-thrust electric trolling motors. Again, eye of the beholder.

Marsh boats do share commonalities, however. Most, if not all, are lightweight, a fact made possible in large part by their fiberglass and flotation foam construction. All are—or at least should be—low profile, easily camouflaged, highly maneuverable, stable, and for the most part, unsinkable.

Layout Boats

Like the sneakboat, the layout boat is a very traditional piece of waterfowling history; however, unlike the sneaker, the layout boat—the MLB or UFO, for example—isn't, at least in my opinion, nearly as versatile. Effective when done correctly? Most definitely,

What About the Dog?

One of the most often-asked questions I get at my waterfowl seminars concerns sneakboats and retrievers. Currently, Julie and I enjoy three black Lab dogs, and I wouldn't think of hunting without at least one of them, even if I'm hunting out of my Canvasback or Aquapod. But what about safety, folks ask? And what about shooting over the dog's head? Very legitimate questions, and I'll address both briefly.

Gun safety is paramount, regardless of whether your hunting partner is human or canine. Establishing safe fields of fire prior to the hunt is a good way to start. Some gunners I've talked with place their retriever behind them in the sneaker. This, they say, accomplishes three things: the dog remains out of the fields of fire; he's concealed in part by the hunter; and finally, his hearing is protected by keeping the muzzle blast away from his ears. An excellent idea in terms of dog placement; however, I want my retrievers to be able to see everything as I see it, and they can't do that from behind.

Whether I'm gunning from the Canvasback or my 10-foot Aquapod, I put my Labs in the bow; *however,* I also position the boat at an angle to the decoy spread, not with the bow pointed directly at the hole or intended landing area. A right-hander, I'll try to position the bow pointing upwind and my left shoulder at the hole. Julie and I have taught our Labs, with the boats on dry ground, to lie steady on the bottom with their chins on the gunwale. This puts us—hound and me—practically side by side, just as if we were sharing a box blind, and with the dog completely hidden by the blind or boat. There are no safety issues, there's no muzzle blast, and Maggie or Jet or Deacon can watch everything as it unfolds. Of course, there will be upwind birds that I have to pass as they enter an area or field of fire to my immediate right; but that's all part of the game.

Clint Robey, Travis Mueller, and Tony Vandemore, aided by their able assistants, set a teal rig in Missouri. Dogs and skiffs go together like ducks and decoys.

Above: John (front) and Mark Rongers of The Mighty Layout Boys anchor a two-man Classic on the Mississippi. *Facing page, top:* Ian McCauley's Missouri-based outfit Momarsh offers a variety of small skiffs, including the Fat Boy pictured here. PHOTO BY CLAY CONNOR *Facing page, bottom: Sculling is an almost forgotten art form within the realm of the waterfowler—sad, because it can be as effective as any tactic employed by the modern gunner.*

but there can be little argument that the layout boat is a specialized skiff.

Though two-gunner layouts are available, the one-man fiberglass boat is by far the most common. Traditional layout boats are battleship gray in color, a hue that closely matches the surface of the water when viewed—as a duck would—from above. This paint scheme, along with the layout boat's extraordinarily low profile and sloped sides, which cause no shadows on the water, are what make the boat so deadly.

Most users will off-load the layout from the tender boat, a larger vessel such as Minchk's high-walled 20-foot LOWE, and anchor it in place first; then, a series of long lines, single lines to which a dozen or more decoys have been clipped, will be arranged according to boat positioning and wind direction. The gunner lies on his back in the bottom of the boat, shoulders slightly elevated, with his fowling piece across his chest. The tender is then anchored some distance upwind, where the captains watch and wait to retrieve downed birds or trade out shooters.

Scull Boats

While I'm certain some will disagree, my thoughts are that of the four types of sneakboats discussed here, it is the scull boat that remains the most unchanged or traditional method of gunning. Scull boats—modern examples being the Hiney, Humboldt, or Merrymeeting Bay models—are long, narrow, sharp-prowed skiffs of either fiberglass or wood. Battleship gray for the same reason as is the layout, scull boats feature low-profile sloping hulls and square transoms.

What's Out There?

If you do a Google search on any of these boats, you're going to find the Internet contains a wealth of information on a wide variety of sneakboats and the hunters who use them. One of the most interesting sites I've found is the Duck Hunters' Boat Page (www.duckboats.net). This incredibly comprehensive site features 'fowlers from around country, and offers up their insight on the best, worst, and most innovative skiffs to ever grace the surface of the water. I find the photography to be most helpful as I, like many duck hunters, am constantly upgrading, enhancing, modifying, and customizing—yeah, it's all screwing around with!—my personal boats, and the images on the pages are just full of great ideas.

Lightweight (#53) and easy-to-handle, the 10-foot Aquapod is an ideal choice for the 'fowler looking for room, comfort, and mobility.

Sneakboats
- Widgeon, Mighty Layout Boys: www.mightylayoutboys.com
- Broadbill & Bluebill, Devlin Boats: www.devlinboat.com
- Blackjack, Arthur Armstrong: www.pokeboat.com
- Classic Barnegat Bay: www.classicbarnegat.com

Marsh boats
- Canvasback, Carstens Industries: www.carstensindustries.com
- Fat Boy and Fat Boy DP, Momarsh: www.momarsh.com
- Aquapod, ATTBAR, Inc.: www.attbar.com
- Stealth 1200, Otter Outdoors: www.otteroutdoors.com

Scull boats
- Hiney scull, Domeyer Scull Boats: www.domeyerscullboats.com
- Merrymeeting Bay scull, the Duck Boat Company: www.tdbco.com
- Brant, Lock, Stock & Barrel: www.waterfowler.net/LS&B
- Sculldugery, Devlin Boats: www.devlinboat.com

Layout boats
- One & two-man layout boats, Mighty Layout Boys: www.mightylayoutboys.com
- UFO layout boat, Waterfowl Works: www.waterfowl-works.com
- Bufflehead, Devlin Boats: www.devlinboat.com

Sculling works like this. After spotting a raft of birds, the sculler wets the hull—the hull and the water's surface now match—and launches from an upwind or up-current location, if possible. The gunner, lying on his back, uses a single long oar extending out from a hole in the transom to propel the skiff toward the flock.

The art of sculling lies in learning to work the oar in the proper figure-8 motion necessary and never letting one's elbow, arm, face—anything—rise above the combing; that is, the top of the hull. Essentially, the scull boat is meant to imitate an unassuming log or other clump of floating debris, and not a man with

Above: Andy Davis and his Hoot ETV (Exteme Terrain Vehicle). A duck skiff? In some situations, most definitely. Right: If you can ride it to your honey hole, set decoys from it, and then use it as a blind, why the hell not?

a firearm intent on doing the birds harm. If everything goes as it should, the sculler paddles, or sculls, into effective shooting range of the rafted birds, rises, and flushes his quarry. Oars, concealed inside the scull boat, are used to return the gunner to the launch site; some enterprising scullers will actually carry small, self-contained outboards with them, which they then put on the transom for the return trip.

Boats are as much a part of the waterfowler's world as are decoys and a good, hard-charging black Lab dog. And while there's absolutely nothing wrong with a 20-foot LOWE, complete with gun lockers, Laz-E-Boy recliners, and hot and cold running water—well, you're just not going to toss that barge in the back of the pickup and launch it off the old railroad grade at the end of the slough, you know, the spot where there's no place to launch a boat, but where all the ducks seem to hang out? Sneakboats aren't a do-all, end-all for today's waterfowler; however, these little skiffs made of fiberglass or wood certainly can save the day, not to mention help make that duck strap hang a little heavier.

CHAPTER 5

The Care and Feeding of Duck and Goose Calls

MY DUCK HUNTING FORMATIVE YEARS were the early 1970s. Back then, my Old Man, Mick, carried with him a hard black plastic OLT D-2 duck call, at that time as traditional an instrument as one might carry afield. The call, to the best of my knowledge, never left the chest pocket of his brown canvas Walls hunting coat, attached, as it were, to the wide wale corduroy collar with a worn piece of rawhide leather and a big safety pin. No . . . I mean it *never* left his pocket. Truth is, I can't honestly remember hearing the Old Man play the call. Maybe once or twice after an hour's worth of 55-cent draft beers at John Shafer's tavern, but never in the field. At the end of the season, he'd hang the OLT up by the rawhide strap from the corner shelf, and there it would remain until mid-October of the next year.

Needless to say, the maintenance required to keep the Old Man's call in working order was minimal; actually, non-existent would more accurate. That, however, isn't the case with every duck hunter's duck call, which brings us to the present, and the topic at hand; namely, how to keep your duck call looking and sounding as it should.

At 36, Iowa's Doug Hess is a waterfowler's waterfowler. A mild-mannered lawn care service owner by day, when he's not trapping moles or cutting grass,

Today's duck and goose calls come in all sorts of shapes, sizes, colors, configurations, and, of course, price ranges.

Hess can be found hard at work at his true passion—duck calling. Five years ago, the young man turned his love of duck-speak into reality, and started River Mallard Calls. Today, Hess offers a full line of wood, acrylic, and polycarbonate duck, goose, and crow calls, all of which are true works of art, both visually and aurally. A most talented craftsman, Hess is a stickler for perfection and performance both in his calls and his landscape technology; as such, constant maintenance and upkeep play key roles in his ability to provide the finest service to his clients, homeowners and duck hunters alike. Knowing this, he seemed a natural to turn to when it came to call care and tuning—I wasn't disappointed.

Left: Polycarbonate calls, such as Hess's goose calls, are a bit more rugged and somewhat less in need of cosmetic maintenance than are traditional wooden calls. **Below:** *Wood calls, however, simply look great—and some say sound better than do those constructed of space-age materials.*

A TROUBLESHOOTING CHART

Think back to the last time you bought a new lawn-mower, Weed-whacker . . . anything. Chances are, it came with instructions, which you probably threw away immediately upon opening the box. If you didn't and you actually read them, there's a good chance those instructions included a troubleshooting chart—a list of problems, possible causes, and potential solutions. "Is there fuel in the fuel tank?" or "Is the appliance plugged into a live electrical outlet?" You know what I'm talking about.

That in mind, let's take a look at what might the world's first duck call troubleshooting chart. Too elemental? Don't laugh; these call-makers see it all the time.

Problem: Call makes no sound at all.

Explanation: Cork and wedge are absent; reed is locked in place.

Solution: "We need to check and make sure that the reed and wedge are in there," says Hess. "If they're there, we need to take the call apart and see if there isn't something wedged underneath the reed that's preventing it from moving. If so, we need to remove that and clean the call. Or is the entire reed and wedge assembly out of whack? If so, we're looking at removing the reed and cork, and starting from scratch."

Problem: The call doesn't sound right.

Explanation: Cork has gotten loose or taken a set; call has been tuned incorrectly by the end-user.

Solution: "A lot of times," says Hess, "we need to replace the cork. That's the most common problem I see. I do try to impress upon people—change your corks often." As Hess explains, true cork can take a set and get loose, or even deteriorate over time, and both can cause the call to change in pitch or tone as the reed gets sloppy. Rubber wedges, too, can be affected by use, time, heat, and other variables. Corks are easy to change and inexpensive; there's no reason *not* to change them. If we have a tuning issue here, the call simply needs to be tuned, and we'll get to that in a moment.

Problem: Call plays, but unexpectedly stops in mid-use.

Explanation: Foreign object wedged between reed and tone board; condensation or moisture in call has frozen; wet reed sticks to tone board.

Calling as well as Californian Paul Beyer does is an art in and of itself. So, too, is maintaining and modifying those calls.

Solution: "Chewing tobacco, weed seeds . . . there's lots of things that get blown into calls that can stop them up," says Hess. "I'd suggest taking the insert out and physically looking to see if there's something under the reed. You can *gently* lift the reed and blow anything out from underneath there, but you want to make sure you don't bend or tweak the reed." Blowing backwards, or via the insert end, into the call can help dislodge any foreign material, too. Water-related problems—ice, excessive moisture, otherwise known as too much spit—can be solved by warming followed by drying. Again, blowing backwards through the call can help.

Problem: Cracked or split reed.

Explanation: This one's pretty obvious—the reed's not well.

Solution: "At the very least, you're looking at replacing the reed," says Hess. "Short of one that's broken, I very seldom replace reeds. A good reed is likely to stay the same; corks, though . . . I'm always changing corks."

Problem: Cork breaks, chips, or gets sloppy; tone of call changes.

Explanation: Again, obvious—the cork's getting up in years.

Solution: "Replace the cork," says Hess. "I always recommend you go back to the guy who made your call, unless you're confident you can do it yourself. You're going to need a rubberized cork. And again, the guy who made your call is going to be able to help you here. A lot of call-makers, especially those making the higher-end calls, will include an extra set or two, reeds and corks."

Note: Hess emphasized this point many times throughout our discussion; that is, if you have any concerns at all about the way your duck call performs, or if you believe it to be in need of repair, you're never wrong to first contact the manufacturer.

Problem: Acrylic or polycarbonate call body cracks, chips, or gets scratched.

Explanation: Regular use or out-and-out abuse—we duck hunters are sometimes tough on gear.

Solution: "There are some techniques for filling, sanding, and rubbing those kinds of marks (i.e. chips, small cracks, scratches) out, but it's an involved process," says Hess. "With scratches, you can either learn to live with it, or perhaps for a small fee, you can send it back to the manufacturer and they might be able to do something with it. As for chips or bigger cracks, you're probably out of luck there." Hess went on to explain that scratches and scuffs on acrylic or polycarbonate calls are "generally aesthetic only," and don't affect the sound of the call.

Problem: Wooden call splits or cracks; finish starts to wear.

Explanation: The wood has remained wet for a length of time, swollen and split; a wet call was dried too quickly, e.g. near a radiator or heat source.

Solution: "If your wood call splits," Hess explains, "it's almost too late to do anything with it. With a finish, if you're handy, you can try to strip the call and refinish it using a polyurethane type of product. It just may be time for another duck call."

NAME THAT TUNE

"Tuning a duck call is simply altering the reed by trimming to achieve the desired sound," says Bill Cooksey. A four-time Tennessee State duck-calling champ, Cooksey's well versed in the art of tuning a call. "Changing the cork is like changing your truck's oil," he says. "It's mandatory maintenance. An accomplished caller can tell when the cork needs changed; we call it 'going flat.' A sure sign is that the call starts to stick (lock up) a lot. But here's what I tell people. Change the cork regularly, and learn to use the call. If you can't blow it to the utmost, there's no sense in you trying to tune it. You can't tune one if you can't blow one."

That all said, here's the bottom line on tuning your duck call. Some call-makers, Hess being one, will spend time with their clients, and walk them through

Four-time Tennessee State duck calling champ and good friend Bill Cooksey, coaxing another bunch into range.
PHOTO BY AVERY PRO-STAFF

Trimming, or as Hess calls it, dog-earing the reed on a duck call. Rule of thumb with tuning: If you can't blow it, you sure as hell shouldn't be tuning it.

the tuning process—how to find the natural bend of the new reed, trimming and cutting, installation, and so on. However, being mechanically capable of altering and installing a new reed, and actually tuning the call as to tone and pitch are, as Hess and others will say, two radically different things. And here, I defer again to Cooksey's advice: If you're a competent caller, you may be a competent tuner. But if you don't know the call, for Heaven's sake don't go cutting on the reed. Either take it or send it back to the man who built it.

ROUTINE CARE AND STORAGE

In truth, there's a good chance that apart from periodically changing out the cork, your duck call won't require any major maintenance. To my way of thinking, scuffs and scratches are a sign of character; that the call is actually used for calling ducks and not simply as part of a costume.

That said, what if the call should need a cleaning mid-season? And what to do with it—sob!—once the season's over? Rinsing a call to get rid of errant weed seeds, bits of Levi Garrett, or that mysteriously missing half a cheeseburger is as elemental a process as is changing a cork. Separate the insert—the half with reed, cork, and tone board—from the barrel, and rinse both under cool running water. "Don't use hot water

to rinse your call," says two-time Nevada duck calling champ Chad Belding. "The heat can possibly affect the mylar reed." Once the call is clean, set the insert and barrel on a towel to air-dry; if you're in a hurry, use lung-power to blow the excess water off. A blow dryer? Bad idea.

End-of-the-season maintenance and storage are all that remain. Following a thorough rinsing inside and out, and complete drying, the two parts of the call can be reassembled. Acrylic or polycarbonate calls, along with the decorative brass bands found on some models, can be polished using any of several commercial compounds; Hess uses Simichrome Polishing Paste (German, imported by Competition Chemicals, Inc., Iowa Falls, IA). Wooden calls should be checked and double-checked for dryness before prolonged storage. "Any carnuba-type wax can be used to polish a finished wooden call," says Hess. "A couple coats not only shine it up, but help protect the wood and finish, too."

In the off-season, store your calls—says Cooksey— someplace where badness won't take place.

Like any fine instrument, a custom call like this SR-1 Paralyzer from Freddie Zink can be mishandled and thrown out of aural whack.

As for storage, everyone's different. "In a perfect world," says Cooksey, "you'd clean the calls up well, and then store them on a shelf or somewhere in the house where the dust will be minimal, the kids can't go to sticking pencils in 'em, or the dogs can't chew 'em up." Because Hess practices and demonstrates his calls year-round, there really isn't any long-term storage in his world, per se. My personal calls get cleaned, go back on the lanyard, and hang in the dry, dehumidified basement until the following September. Perfect? Perhaps not, but I know that come the opener, those same calls will sound as they did the day I took them out of the package. Now, if only I could play them like Hess and Cooksey. . . .

THE HORROR OF IT ALL

Years ago, my grandparents owned and operated a small sporting goods store in my hometown of Newton Falls, Ohio. As part of the family-owned business, my father—their eldest son and an avid angler—was put in charge of reel repair. "The absolute worst thing you could see," he told me on several occasions, "was for a man to walk into the shop carrying a paper grocery sack." When I asked why, he would grimace, take another drag on his Camel Light, and say "Because

you could be damn sure that in that bag were the parts of a fishing reel that this guy had taken apart and couldn't get back together. Or he'd gotten it back together wrong and it didn't work." Twenty years later, he can laugh about it; he didn't laugh much about it then.

I tell this story with a purpose, my purpose being that duck calls and fishing reels have a lot in common when it comes to shade tree mechanics and all-thumbs try-it-yourselfers. That is, there's been more than one duck call disassembled in the name of tuning or cleaning or polishing or what-have-you, only to have to be carried into the local sporting goods store in a paper sack by a red-faced "I don't ask directions" male with a hangdog look and a thousand excuses. And it'll happen again.

So with this in mind, I asked a handful of call-makers and hardcore callers to tell me one of their favorite—or as the case as often been, least favorite—horror stories dealing with the man, the paper sack, and the duck call that . . . well, that's seen better days.

Warning: These stories are presented as they've been told. You folks with weak stomachs might want to think twice, or have a bottle of Rolaids ready. . . .

Scott Threinen: Competitive goose caller, Avery Pro-Staff, all-round good kid

I was out in the parking lot practicing for a calling contest that was about to start when a buddy came running out the door looking for me. I asked him what happened, and he said he just blew the reed out of his call and wondered if I could retune if for him. Just minutes before the contest started, I said, "Give it here." As a note, I knew he chewed a lot, and I don't think he had brushed his teeth since last Arbor Day.

So I took the call from him and opened it up. This guy had so much chew spit in there that when I opened it, spit just started pouring out from both ends. It went all over my hands and down my pants. Man, I just dropped the call, and when I dropped it on the concrete, it busted into a million pieces. He started yelling at me and I started yelling at him. It was so gross that to this day if I ever take a guy's call apart, I ask them if they chew *and* then I tip it upside down. The funny thing was, this guy ended up using his hunting call and getting third in the contest. He told me afterwards that the call felt more "freed up." Gross!

Chad Belding: Entrepreneur, competitive caller, comedian

I met "Bill" at a calling contest in May of 2004. He was just hanging out, trying to pick up some of the new notes that were being laid down on stage. I was introduced to him through a mutual friend, and he began to tell me how he had been blowing a short reed call for about eight months and he was really making progress with it. He then told me that lately he wasn't getting the same sounds out of his call as he was when he first got it. I asked him what type of call, he told me, and I said I'd take a look at it if he wanted me to. That was my first mistake. His eyes lit up like a Christmas tree as he rushed off to his truck. Usually it takes me about ten minutes to assess the situation and get a call back in working order, but that wasn't going to be the case here.

So "Bill" tries to hand me his call, but it stuck to his hand. He had obviously spilled some sort of soda or something on it. I grabbed it with my thumb and finger, and went to my booth to see what I could do. I tried to pull the two pieces apart, but they were not about to move. I even had my brother, Clay, try for a minute but we finally decided to take it inside the store to run it under some water.

After I got it warmed up a bit, it finally began to open. Now I realize that buffets are popular in Nevada but I couldn't believe the assortment of food inside his call; man, the food was everywhere. I had to plug my nose the entire time because of the smell. There were pieces of M&Ms, roast beef, bread, jerky, Copenhagen, and what looked to be lettuce.

So it was back into the store to wash the call. Twenty minutes later, I returned to get this thing tuned for him. I shaved him a brand new reed, inserted two new O-rings, and added a little tape to his stopper. I handed it back to him, and he went to town on it. Finally, he looked at me and told me it would do.

Nevada's Chad Belding, a competitive goose caller, makes some modifications to a unit that, to him, just didn't sound right. PHOTO BY AVERY PRO-STAFF

He shook my hand and told me the last thing that I wanted to hear: "If I run into another problem with it," he said, "I'll give you a call." Perfect!

Bill Saunders: Call-maker, killer of small Canadas, walleye fisherman

One of the funniest things I saw actually happened to a call of mine. Growing up, I was a Tim Grounds guy, and owe much of my success to Tim and his calls. Anyway, I had a pet Half-Breed—that's a goose call, not a dog—in a Mossy Oak pattern that had nearly all the camo worn off from being in my hand so much. I'm telling you the geese could not resist this call. It had the sweetest tune you had ever heard, and I refused to touch it fearing I would mess it up.

One day, I looked in the exhaust end of the call to see what was so magical about it, and noticed there was something in it. Upon closer inspection, I found a green sprout of some kind that had obviously germinated from a seed lodged between the wedge and the hand piece. I had blown the call so much, keeping it warm and safe in my coat that I had grown that little seed with the warmth of my breath. The day finally came, though, when I had to take the call apart to replace a split reed, and the little sprout was removed, but not before we had two cuttings of alfalfa of it.

And final note. As a call maker, I would like to see more guys wash their calls out before they send them in. The sight and smell of chew, sunflower seeds, and coffee all mixed into a call and aged is very—let's call it—undesirable.

Field Hudnall: Call designer/maker, videographer, member of ZINK Calls Team, World Champion goose caller

One retune job that sticks out in my mind more than others was when I was working a retail event for one of our vendors. There was a young man that I kept talking with about goose calling. He told me he had a call from another maker he was having trouble with, and asked me to retune it for him. I told him no problem—I don't mind tuning someone's calls no matter who the maker.

So he goes out to the truck to get the call. On his return, I noticed he filled his lip with one of the largest dips of Copenhagen I have ever seen in one man's lip. I don't dip and I don't I have a problem with it, but I

could see where this was going. Before he handed me the call, he insisted on demonstrating how out of tune it was. When he pulled the call away from his lip, he had a dribble of spit running down his chin. As I took the call apart, tobacco spit dripped out of the end of the call—the reed was stained brown and covered with grains of tobacco. The whole time I was taking the call apart, the young man kept telling me hunting stories and watching me work on his call.

After I separated the reed from the tone channel and cleaned the river of spit from it, I shaved a new reed. I wiped the call down with an alcohol swab and cleaned it up as best as I could. I put it back together, blew it a couple times, and handed it back. "There you go," I said, "it's sounding good now."

He blew the call for about two minutes, handed it back, and said, "Nahhh. Can you make 'er a little lighter?" As he's handing the call back, now, he's wiping his chin again. Needless to say, the call had been nicely replanted with good 'ol Copenhagen Long Cut.

I laughed. What can you do?

Gentleman "farmer," Bill Saunders. Read, and you'll understand.

Goose calling champ and awfully nice kid, Field Hudnall (left), takes some time to walk photographer Bill Buckley through an impromptu lesson.

Barnie Calef: World Champion duck caller, creator of Calef Calls

In my first year of competition, I was off to Springfield, Illinois, for a regional contest. After arriving, this fellow approaches me and asks if I was affiliated with the call he was blowing. I said I was, and he proceeds to pull his call out of his jacket pocket. I couldn't believe my eyes when sand just poured out. He hands it to me and says, "It doesn't sound right."

I thought to myself, "Imagine that. A wooden duck call blown full of sand not sounding right." I figured the call would be ruined by the reed pounding all that sand into the tone board, but decided to give it a go—just to see what shape it truly was in. So I pull the insert out of the barrel to clean it up, and quickly decide that the sand is the least of my problem. Somewhere along the line, the guy had decided he was a call maker, and had cut the exhaust bore, in his words, "a little deeper and wider." I don't know what he thought it would accomplish, but it was evident that he discovered his mistake. He had taken a piece of pine, and had fashioned a small dam across the newly enlarged bore. I had to tell him that he had ruined the call and there was nothing to do but replace it.

We still talk about that one.

CHAPTER 6

Mysteries of the Blind Bag

BEFORE WE GET STARTED, ALLOW ME JUST a minute to explain what's happening here. Over the course of the next few pages, you're going inside the blind bags of some of the nation's finest duck and goose hunters. I'm sure you'll recognize more than a few of these gentlemen. Their names are synonymous with waterfowling east to west. Others are up-and-comers; the next generation, so to speak, and you'd be wise to keep a close eye on these young guns. You never know where the next Tim Grounds or Freddie Zink's going to show up, now do you?

So step inside. Shine a light into the darkest corners, and see in their words what helps make these men the best in their chosen field. And why. Go on . . . scratch your head and ask yourself, "Now why didn't I think of that?" Or in some cases, "What the hell?" Either way, one thing's for sure; it's going to be an interesting ride.

OUR PRO, CHAD BELDING
My name is Chad Belding—date of birth: October 10, 1974—and I'm from Reno, Nevada. I own and operate a couple of construction site service companies, including a portable restroom company, and an environmental street sweeping company. I also work full time for

The contents of the modern waterfowler's blind bag isn't that mysterious—or is it?

Avery Outdoors dealing with their western promotions. I guess you could say I'm a toilet pumper during the summer, and a waterfowler during the fall.

I drive an '06 Ford F-250 diesel because I need the power. I'm into playing ping-pong and watching baseball, and try to catch at least one episode of the *Sopranos* every week, even if it's a rerun.

Competitive calling history: I won the Nevada State Duck Calling title in 2003, and again in 2005, and have won the Nevada State goose calling title three times now. I've called in Stuttgart at the World Duck Championships three times. According to the website www.callingducks.com, I'm ranked in the top 20 among the country's goose callers. I've placed in the top five in over twenty goose calling competitions, and have placed second in sixteen different contests. Ah, well. . . .

Pet waterfowl gun and load: I shoot a Benelli Super Black Eagle II, with a Patternmaster choke tube and Hevi-Shot #2s.

Blind bag of choice: Avery Floating Blind Bag. I know for a fact the bag floats because mine ended up floating in Tindell's Reservoir outside of Stuttgart, Arkansas. Everything made it home safe, except for my two cell phones and my turkey sandwiches. To this day, I have no idea how the bag ended up in the water.

Reason for being: Before every hunt, I pray to God for a safe hunt and a good time. Myself, I'm in it for the good times, the sunrises, the friendships, the family bonds, and the birds themselves. In my life, it's always waterfowl season.

Belding's Blind Bag Revealed
Hevi-Shot #2s—I use them for both ducks and geese.
Chapstick—The cherry flavor's the best.
Handwarmers—I have weak skin on my hands, and they get cold easily.
Snack bars and/or protein bars
Avery DIY call lanyard with Zink Calls' LM (Little Man)-1, SR-1, XR-2, and Power Hen

If Larry the Cable Guy had a brother from whom he was separated at birth, that brother would be this man—Chad Belding. PHOTO BY AVERY PRO-STAFF

Extra reeds for each of the calls

Extra duck and goose calls—Sometimes the birds want to hear something different.

Avery and Zink Calls skull caps—I hate when my ears and neck get cold, so I combine the skull caps with a neck gaiter, and stay nice and warm. Plus, the skull caps don't get in the way in a Power Hunter or a pit like a billed cap can.

Avery fleece neck gaiter—Best product the company makes.

Avery Floating Suck [sic] Strap—Author's note: Any time I have the opportunity to get on Belding's case about anything, I do. Here, I'm assuming the young man means duck strap. It's odd, certainly, but not as strange as when Scott Thrienen, '02 Minnesota State goose calling champion, wrote me his blind bag list, which included the sentence: "Snakes. You always need snakes." What the boy meant was snacks; his fingers just got in the way of his typing. Same with Belding.

Avery caller's gloves—A must for every duck and goose caller.

Three Diet Cokes—Why diet? I believe in eating my calories, not drinking them.

Hunting licenses

Asthma medicine and inhaler—Working flocks makes me wheeze.

Beef, goose, or deer jerky

Binoculars—Compact, of course.

Digital camera—I won't leave the house without my digital camera in my bag. It's actually more important than the gun.

Extra pair of socks—You just never know.

Dog trainer controller—He knows when he has the collar on, and I never have to push the button.

Dog treats—Overlooked by many, but shouldn't be.

OUR PRO, BILL SAUNDERS

For background, Saunders, who currently lives in the eastern Washington goose-hunting hotbed of Kennewick, provided the following: "Date of birth is June 29, 1972. My wife's name is Lorri; her age is top secret. I have two daughters—Kelsie, who's ten, and Amanda, who's seven. I drive a white Dodge 2500 4x4, with Marathon MAX-4 seat covers—best-ever investment for a truck. When I'm not hunting, I spend as much time as possible with my family doing normal things.

Washington's Bill Saunders—call-maker, family man, and, when he's not goose hunting, avid walleye fisherman.
PHOTO BY BILL SAUNDERS

I fish salmon and walleye as much as possible, and love watching the Green Bay Packers, Seattle Mariners, and Gonzaga basketball. I have two retrievers—Nash, 13, is retired, and Shaq, 2. Both were trained by Tab Smith at Goose Pit Kennels. Tab is my kinda trainer; he spends a ton of time in the field, and knows what a hunter really needs."

Why I hunt: I'm not good at anything else.

Pro-Staff affiliations: Final Approach (FA Brand) and the Drake Elite Team.

Guiding and competitive calling history: I work as a full-time guide in eastern Washington at Pacific Wings, and have done that for about ten years now. I figure I hunt around 125 days a year or so. As for the competitive calling, I have over twenty-five first-place finishes, including three-time Washington State goose calling champion, four-time Pacific Flyway Regional Champion, and three-time Final Approach Champ. I have had a ton of fun and success contest calling, but nothing compares to the real deal: hunting!

Guide Series Calls history: I started building calls in 1999. My wife told me that I had to get a real job when I wasn't guiding, but that wasn't an option for me. Now, several years later, the call business has turned into more of a real job than I could have ever imagined. Today, we build several different Canada, speck, snow, brant, and duck calls, and we feel we offer the finest calls for the field. (Author's note: Saunders does build some dandy calls, all of which can be seen at www.guideseriescalls.com.)

Pet shotgun and ammunition: Winchester Super X2 in a 12-gauge, with a light Modified choke. Ammunition is 3-inch Kent BBs.

Blind bag of choice: I use two types of bags, both in MAX-4. The first one is a Final Approach (FA) All-Season gear bag. I use this one when I guide as it's large enough to carry everything I need. The second one is a small FA Gunner Bag, and I use this when I have to pack into my hunting location.

Saunders's Blind Bag Revealed

Two boxes of 1¹/₈ ounce, 3-inch Kent BBs for both ducks and geese—My favorite quote is "It's not the arrow; it's the Indian."

Can of Break-Free Gun Lube—This has saved many days.

Leatherman Multi-Tool—I think you could build a house with this one.

Staple gun and two boxes of staples—This is a must for every pit hunter.

Pair of leather gloves—I try not to use these if I can help it.

FA Brand neck gaiter—A must before your whiskers grow in.

Bottle of ibuprofen

Mag-lite

Bag of Dill Pickle SPITZ sunflower seeds

Hunting regs with shooting times

Two hundred feet of decoy cord with swivel—For a jerk cord.

Roll of toilet paper—Socks aren't cheap!

Small first aid kit—I didn't start bringing this until a few years ago, but it's now one of the most important things I carry.

Goose calls—Two Traffics, one wood and one acrylic; a poly-carb Reload; and an I-5 KLR

Duck calls-Two Gravity duck calls

OUR PRO, KELLEY POWERS

Volunteer State native, Kelley Powers, gave me the following insider information: "Born on July 17, 1978. I drive a green 2003 Chevrolet Silverado EXT Z71 that rides like a car, but is rugged like a truck. Retriever? HR Final Flight's Sur Shot—though I call him Champ—was two years old in July, and trained by Sur-Shot Retrievers and Mr. Jimmy McMahan. As for what I'm doing when I'm *not* hunting, there's turkey hunting—wait, that's hunting, too. I do enjoy fishing, shooting trap, and graphic design. And why I hunt? I enjoy the camaraderie of being with family and friends, and watching the birds work and respond to the calling."

Pro-Staff affiliations: Winchester Ammunition; Drake Waterfowl Elite Team; Higdon Decoys; Tim Grounds Championship Calls; Triton Boats; E.A.R., Inc.; Waterfowler TV Elite Team; Go-Devil Motors.

Guiding and competitive calling history: I have my own full-scale duck and goose hunting guide service

Tennessee's Kelley Powers working the magic on a flock of southern honkers. PHOTO BY KELLEY POWERS

down here in Tennessee called Final Flight Outfitters (www.finalflight.com).

Author's note: As for Powers's competitive calling history, it—like that of all of the young men featured in this column—is incredibly impressive, to say the least. Kelley, again like them all, has enjoyed this success in part due to the fantastic support and encouragement of many, including, and perhaps most significantly, his family. That said, Powers' resume' includes:

World Goose Calling champion
World Goose Calling Champion of Champions
International Goose Calling champion
Worldwide Goose Calling champion
World Open Goose Calling champion
Two-time U.S. Open champion
North American Masters champion
Two-time World Team Goose Calling champion
Two-time World Open "Meat" Duck Calling champion

Call business history: I designed a Canada goose call, as well as a snow/speck call for Rich-n-Tone Calls. And I recently launched the design of the Kelley Powers Triple Crown goose call. This one is an exact replica of the modified Tim Grounds Super Mag call that I've used in contests since 1998. This call's greatest feature is the tone board—an exact mold of the worn-in-set that I have used on stage for years.

Television, film, and video history: I've done outdoor productions for ESPN, The Nashville Network, The Men's Network, and The Outdoor Channel. My video appearances have include Rich-n-Tone's "Power Trip," and numerous Tim Grounds hunting and instructional productions.

Pet shotgun and ammunition: A Browning Gold, with a PatternMaster Choke and Winchester Supreme ammunition.

Blind bag of choice: Drake Waterfowl Systems Floating Blind Bag, large.

Powers's Blind Bag Revealed

Winchester Supreme shells
Four feet of bungee cord and decoy twine—Perfect for those still days when you need a jerk cord. This has been a lifesaver in the past. Every blind bag should have this just in case you need it, and especially if you're hunting new spots.

Maui Jim sunglasses
Carmex medicated lip balm
Old pair of decoy gloves
Pair of leather gloves for driving the boat
Gerber multi-tool—You just never know when you're going to need it.
Kill tags—Our outfitting business has kill tags for all our customers' birds. After the hunt, these tags keep limits separate and organized instead of putting the birds in individual piles.
Pens—For filling out the kill tags.
Cell phone—Do you really think that I'd leave home without it? Also comes in handy for finding out how the other hunters are doing.
GPS—Some spots are hard to find in the dark, and this comes in awful handy.
SportDog Wetland Hunter Dog Collar—For Champ.

OUR PRO, FIELD HUDNALL

Born in Louisville on January 7, 1981. I'm from LaGrange, Kentucky, so my parents, grandparents, and other relatives all live in the great state of Kentucky. My older brother, Clay, lives and works with me in Ohio, and he's not only my brother, but my best friend. I hope to be married some day and raise a family of my own, but right now, I have an awesome girlfriend who does put up with my crazy lifestyle.

The Crazy Lifestyle: I moved to Ohio four years ago to begin work with Fred Zink and Zink Calls. I've lived with Fred and his wife, Dawn, since that time, but we're now preparing to move the company to Port Clinton (Ohio), where Clay and I are planning to buy our own place.

I've worked with Zink Calls since August 2002. Every year, we work on new call designs; our latest is the Money Maker, which is my signature series call that Fred and I designed for me to use in competition. I've used this one for all my major wins, and it's been a hit with beginning goose callers due to its ease of operation.

I wear quite a few hats at Zink Calls—tuning custom calls, director of video productions, Creative Marketing manager, product development, sponsorship overseer, and others. One of the hardest things is explaining just exactly what I do there. I don't have much free time, but I do love my work—so it's worth it to me.

Competitive calling history: I've been very fortunate to win some prestigious calling contests, but all I can say is it was all luck. I was lucky to have Carl Lausman (Lausman Game Calls) in the beginning. My parents are very supportive and encouraging, and my Mom, who's awesome, actually drove me across several states in order to compete. And I've been lucky to spend time with Fred, who gave me all the tools and instruction I needed to be competitive. I believe in giving credit where credit's due, and I wouldn't have won these championships had it not been for these folks.

Author's note: Hudnall's calling resume reads like the *Who's Who of Goose Calling*. His wins include, in part: 2005 Winchester World Open Goose; 2005 International Invitational Goose; 2004 World Goose; 2004 World Live Duck; 2004 North American Two-man Goose; 2004 Bass Pro/Redhead Open Goose; 2003 and 2005 Ohio State Goose Calling Champion; 2003 Canadian-American International Two-Man Goose; and on and on and on. The boy's won a ton!

Pet shotgun and load: I shoot a Benelli Super Black Eagle or a Remington 870, either filled with three-inch Hevi-Shot #2 (geese) or #4 (ducks). As a member of the Wad Wizard Choke Tubes pro-staff, I also shoot a WW Supreme tube, both for ducks and geese in the fall, and turkeys in the spring.

Blind bag of choice: Finisher Blind Bag (Avery Outdoors). The bag fits me 'cause it holds everything I take into the field in one compact unit. I like smaller blind bags because they'll fit inside the blind without taking up too much room.

Reason for being: Hunting is something that gets in your blood; it's a common bond. An ex-girlfriend once told me that I had a problem. [Author's note: Don't all waterfowlers?] She told me I couldn't be friends with anyone who didn't hunt. I disagreed, but she did have a point. I *can* be friends with someone who doesn't hunt, but we'll never share that common ground. Hunting, for me, helps foster a special bond between family and between friends that non-hunters, unfortunately, will never experience.

Hudnall's Blind Bag Revealed

Binoculars

Head lamp

Quick cutters/speed saw—Great for cutting brush for blinds.

If you look up the phrase "damn nice kid" in the dictionary, there's a good chance that Field Hudnall's picture will be right there next to it. PHOTO BY AVERY PRO-STAFF

Fleece callers gloves

Small knife

Zip-Loc bag with toilet paper and matches—Toilet paper for obvious reasons, but it also makes a great fire-starter. You never know when you might have boat trouble, and have to stay the night somewhere.

Two Game Hog game straps

Neoprene Powerbelt shell carrier

Fleece neck gaiter and skull cap

Extra reeds—I carry extra reeds which are already tuned for the different pitches I might need; it saves room rather than carrying extra calls.

Bottle of water

Dr. Pepper, 20-ouncer—I hate coffee, but need the caffeine.

Gummy bears, one bag—I have a sweet tooth, and gummy bears won't get rock hard like a candy bar will.

Beef jerky, one bag—Filling, and loaded with protein.

Extra neoprene ankle gaiters—In case your buddy forgot his, do some trading.

GPS—Great for finding the X in the dark.

Extra gloves—I like the cheap brown work gloves you can buy at the gas station.

A couple extra strap weights—You never know when you're going to have a weight break away.

Ten feet of string or parachute cord—You can use it to help construct a blind, tie down a dog, rig a decoy, anything.

OUR PRO, TONY VANDEMORE

I grew up in northwest Illinois, where my father and uncle began taking me to the blind when I was still in diapers. I grew up hunting geese on farm ponds and in agricultural fields, and hunted ducks with my grandfather who was a member of two duck clubs in the famed Illinois River Bottoms. Many of my childhood afternoons were also spent pheasant and quail hunting with friends.

I attended college in Kirksville, Missouri, at Truman State University, where I received a BS degree in business marketing. The area was, and is, rich with outdoor opportunities and I loved it. After a stint in the San Diego Padres farm system, I returned to Missouri, putting my degree to work as a commercial insurance agent.

Vandemore in the 21st Century: Today, I live in Kirksville, Missouri, with my 4½-year-old black lab, Ruff. I hunt ducks, geese, and turkeys throughout the Central and Mississippi flyways. As a Flyway Manager for Avery Outdoors, I oversee the Pro-Staffers in the Mississippi Flyway; I'm also a member of the Zink Calls Z-Unit Team. I am blessed with the opportunity to spend a lot of days in the field between the beginning of September and the end of May, and this allows me the opportunity to test a lot of products and take a lot of photos.

Duck and goose calls of choice: Zink PowerHen—excellent tonal range, pure duck on the bottom end and still has great top end; Zink LM-1—one of the most versatile calls on the market, very fast and responsive, it's a higher pitched call, but both little geese and big geese alike eat it up.

Pet shotgun and load: Benelli Super Black Eagle with a Terror extended choke tube. It's one of the original ones. I put over eight cases [Author's note: Boys, that's 2,000 rounds] of waterfowl loads through it last season without cleaning it, and it never missed a lick! The Remington Wingmaster HD is pretty lethal stuff!

For ducks I prefer the 3-inch #4s, and for geese I prefer the 3-inch BBs.

Blind bag of choice: The Avery Power Hunter Blind Bag. This bag is great for the hunter who needs to be mobile. It has a shoulder strap and satchel design which makes it comfortable to carry. I used to carry one of the big Avery Pit Bags and it was loaded, but I found that with a little thought I could pack the smaller bag for a particular hunt and not have to carry extra and unneeded weight. Some of my holes are way off the road, and the smaller bag is great for long walks. I also like it because it fits easily inside my layout blind.

Vandemore's Blind Bag Revealed

Avery DIY Lanyard and Calls (I usually only take four calls to the field), two Zink Power Hen duck calls tuned differently, a Zink LM-1 goose call, and a Zink PM-1 goose call.

Replacement guts and reeds—When you split a reed halfway through the hunt, you are back in business in no time.

Tony Vandemore of Kirksville, Missouri, is as good an all-round hunter as I've met in my 35 years afield.

Avery Game Hog Game Strap—I'm all about sunrises, but hopefully I'll be packing something out when the hunt is done; a game strap makes it a lot easier.

Nikon D80 digital camera—I love taking photos during and after the hunts. It's nice to preserve those memories in a photo album.

Avery fleece neck gaiter—An invaluable piece of gear for me!

Fleece skull caps—I usually carry a white one for the snowy conditions, and a camo one for all others. When I'm hunting out of a layout blind, I don't like the bill of my hat catching on the doors and getting knocked off. The skull caps are the answer.

Avery neoprene handwarmer—I don't care to wear gloves when it is cold. The neoprene handwarmer keeps my hands warm in between bunches and between picking up decoys. It also has a little storage room for a candy bar, a pair of sunglasses, etc.

Remington Wingmaster HD ammunition—4s for ducks and BBs for geese.

Avery power flag—A goose hunter's best friend; never leave home without a flag.

Dogtra 1200NCP Electronic Collar

Avery 24-inch trainers lead and coated dog collar—Breaking dogs are a danger to themselves and other hunters. The trainer's lead has a built-in quick release buckle so after the shot and things have settled down, you can quickly release your dog.

Ziploc bag of Eukanuba Premium Performance dog food—Conditions can get brutal throughout the season in areas I hunt, so when spending long days afield in extreme temps, I give Ruff a little snack every now and then to help keep his energy up.

EMT gel—Hard-charging dogs are all the time getting nicks and cuts. I keep a full vet first-aid kit in the truck.

Bottled water—I always pack at least one bottle of water for the dog when dry field hunting; more if it is really hot out.

Avery whistle lanyard and whistle—Unfortunately, I do a pretty fair job of breaking and losing equipment. The back up whistle in the bag has come in handy on more than one occasion.

Avery Neo-Bottle—Hunting season wears on you; I got to have my coffee!

Buck fixed blade knife—Not sure on the model. I got it when I was just a kid, and often wonder how many birds and animals it has seen in the twenty or so years I have had it.

OUR PRO, ALEX LANGBELL

I started hunting in my home state of Nevada when I was 11 years old—shot my first duck at 12. After graduation, I packed an old Ford Ranger and a U-Haul trailer, and moved up to Washington State. Following

Another eastern Washingtonian, Alex Langbell, is co-owner of the well recognized outfitting service Columbia Basin Waterfowl. PHOTO BY ALEX LANGBELL

two years of competitive testing, I began a career as a firefighter for the city of Yakima. Today, I make my home in the Tri-Cities with my wife Andrea, and daughter, Madison. In the Cities, I met veteran waterfowl hunting guides, Craig Riche, and Steve Shultz, and together we formed Columbia Basin Waterfowl, a guide service and video production company. In addition to my roles as a waterfowl guide and videographer, I also serve on the Avery Outdoors and Zink Calls pro-staff teams.

The Langbell Hounds: Two dogs currently—a Chesapeake Bay retriever named Jake, and a yellow Lab name of Gauge. I love 'em all, but have a weakness for the Chessies.

Pet shotgun and ammunition: I shoot several different shotguns over the course of the season, but my favorite is (Craig) Riche's Beretta Silver Mallard. As for ammunition, I'm exclusively a Kent man, with high-velocity—that's 1,560 fps!—three-inch steel getting the nod.

Blind bags of choice: I use a pair of Avery Pro-Grade bags for my professional video equipment, as well as for equipment for filming. One bag has the camera, spare batteries, extra lens, microphone, cables, tapes, and several other accessories. An expandable guide bag holds my large camera batteries and cords, especially when the weather turns cold and I need a little more room.

I have an Avery camera bag, which has my digital camera, spare battery for the digital, flash, and lenses. In a Finisher bag goes all my hunting gear.

Langbell's Blind Bag Revealed

Kent Fast-Steel shotshells

Lanyard with three Zink LM-1s—One is tuned for bigger Western honkers, one tuned for little cacklers, and the last tuned for lesser.

Gerber Multi-plier

Gun lubricant and cloth

Stapler and staples—For touching up pit lids with cover (corn stubble, tumbleweeds, etc.).

Chemical toe warmers

Fleece skull cap

Aspirin

Leather work gloves—For pulling prickly tumbleweeds apart to cover layout blinds.

Napkins—For wiping both ends.

Food and bottled water

Now living near Sacramento, southeastern transplant Curt Wilson is currently the two-time California State goose calling champ.

OUR PRO, CURT WILSON

I'm originally from southwestern Kentucky—the river bottoms off the Mississippi, actually—but now live in Oroville, California, which is about 60 miles north of Sacramento. My dad started me out hunting, and ducks quickly became my passion—I can still remember those early mornings hovering around that old charcoal bucket to keep warm. Reelfoot Lake was my waterfowling home back then; it's where I really learned to call ducks and geese. I moved out to California a couple years back, and currently serve as the Western Territory Manager for Avery Outdoors.

It doesn't matter if you carry a blind bag or a Ziploc bag; what matters is that you have what you need to get the job done. Do you?

Competitive calling history: To tell the truth, I started contest calling to improve my own skills. I've had a handful of goose calling victories in Oklahoma, Texas, Tennessee, and most recently in my home state of California. I've won the California State Goose Calling Contest the past two years (2005–2006).

Pet shotgun and load: Believe it or not, I'm still shooting the same trusty shotgun that I got when I was 16 years old; I'm 33 now. That 870 has been used to break ice, paddle the boat and kill many turkeys, ducks, and geese. Last year the gun hit the sandy floor of Humboldt Bay while I was hunting black brant. It filled with sand and salt water, but after flushing it out with a bottle of fresh water, the gun shot fine the rest of the day.

Reason for being: I wouldn't say that I have an area of expertise in waterfowling, but I can tell you my favorite way to hunt ducks—flooded timber. Unfortunately, that kind of hunting is hard to come by here in the West; however, there's plenty of dry field hunting available, and there's just something about fooling ducks and geese into your spread in those dry fields.

Blind bag of choice: Avery Outdoors Finisher blind bag in Nat-Gear camo. It's big enough to take everything I need, but small enough not to weigh me down.

Wilson's Blind Bag Revealed

Kent Fasteel in 3-inch #2 shot

Bottled water

Headlamp with extra batteries

Bug spray—Early season.

Snacks—You never know how long the hunt will last, and I'd rather go prepared than go hungry.

Avery Neo-Bottle filled with coffee

Selection of Zink Calls—XR-2 and Power Hen duck calls; Moneymaker, Little Man, and Power Speck goose calls.

Leatherman multi-tool—You never know when you're going to have to take your gun apart or steal a band off your buddy's duck.

Extra pair of socks
Cell phone

Pro's note: It's not in my blind bag, but my camera goes with me on every hunt. I try to make sure that I capture the hunt on film, so that others can enjoy it as much as I did.

OUR PRO, LAMAR BOYD

My name's Lamar Boyd, 22, and I'm from Tunica, Mississippi. Currently, I'm a senior at Mississippi State University who slips away from time to time to do a little duck hunting.

I was introduced to the wonderful world of duck hunting by my father, Mike. When I was in tenth grade, I guided my first group of clients for my father, who owns Beaver Dam Hunting Services. [Author's note: For those few who don't recognize the name, Beaver Dam is that most hallowed ground made notable by legendary outdoor writer, Nash Buckingham.]

I don't consider myself an expert by any means, but I do consider myself somewhat knowledgeable when it comes to hunting flooded cypress sloughs and oxbows such as Beaver Dam. I know no other hunting than this, and that's all right with me— I love every minute of it.

Pet shotgun and load: I shoot a Beretta AL 390 Silver Mallard, 12-gauge, in black and synthetic, with a Modified choke. The choke's partially due to the fact that it hasn't been out in years, and won't come out. It's fine, though, as most of our shooting in the holes is pretty close. As for ammunition, I'm using Remington's Nitro-Steel in a three-inch $1\frac{1}{4}$-ounce load of #2s.

The dog: My retriever is a four-year-old male black Lab named Hoss. Like me, he hasn't competed much, but he is a finished dog with hand signals and all that good stuff; his main job is to retrieve ducks. I also hunt with my dad's female black Lab, Molly, quite a bit. She's a veteran, no-nonsense, and makes quick work of her duties.

Boyd's Blind Bag Revealed

Everything I carry into the field gets there in my Avery Outdoors Floating Pit Bag in Mossy Oak Break-Up. I can carry plenty of junk, and the bag's rugged and functionally simplistic. I'll have with me:

Haydel's Cajun Squeal duck call—A double reed call that produces a good ducky sound that suits my taste.
Citrus-flavored Tums—About as unusual as I get. Supper and/or breakfast can sometimes be a little painful.
Bottle of Rem-Oil
Three Streamlight lights, including their Scorpion and Poly-Stinger models.
Snap-ring pliers—They work really well for removing (duck) bands without having to cut the leg of the bird.
Selection of Avery neck gaiters and skull caps
Avery Neo-Bottle with coffee—For when the Diet Coke runs out or freezes up.
Sport-Dog collar transmitter

Lamar Boyd, along with his father, Mike, run Beaver Dam Guide Service out of Tunica, Mississippi. Both father and son are extremely good people.

CHAPTER 7

Cyber-Scouting and Today's Waterfowler

CYBER-SCOUTERS. INTERNET EXPLORERS. Spot-stealers. Unethical, lazy, rotten, duck-nabbin' @&%<+*!#@!! They're known by myriad names, these computerized individuals who, rumor has it, lurk around the fringes of popular websites devoted to waterfowl and waterfowl hunting, their only reason for existence being to discover, electronically, the location of your favorite duck hole, and then go there. Repeatedly.

But is that all there is to it, this cyber-scouting? This supposed high-tech thievery? Or can the Internet and its wealth of electronic riches actually help you become a better, more efficient waterfowler? Where does traditional scouting, for lack of a better phrase, stop, and spot-nabbing begin? Climb on aboard the Information Superhighway, and let's take a look around the waterfowling community, where at times hardware and hardcore clash.

CYBER-SCOUTING = SPOT THIEVERY?
In December of 2005, the Washington State forum, a part of The Duck Hunter's Forum (duckhunter.net), featured a thread—a story title, that is—specifically addressing the subject of Internet scouting. Does it happen? Is it detrimental? And the biggie: Has anyone

Advice on topics such as dog training situations, and improvements in gear and tactics can all be uncovered via the Internet. PHOTO BY AVERY PRO-STAFF

Resourceful individual, or underhanded godless heathen? And what is an Internet scouter, anyway?

been burnt, or had their favorite duck hunting hole ravaged and pillaged unmercifully by an unscrupulous public, as a result of information posted and later retrieved from an Internet website?

The results, as you can view for yourself, varied widely. In Reader's Digest Condensed form, these included comments ranging from "I've been burnt" to "It's bad," "It's not prevalent," and "What's the difference?" and my personal favorite and a theory to which I subscribe wholeheartedly—"If you're going to post photographs of dead ducks with recognizable landmarks available of a public location on a public forum, then you should expect an increase in the popularity of that particular spot." In other words, if you're going to sit in the middle of the train tracks, there's an awfully good chance that you and Mister Burlington Northern will meet.

What was perhaps more interesting than the comments themselves was the amount of attention this particular subject garnered. Throughout its run, the "Internet Scouting" thread mustered 73 full-fledged responses and an astonishing 2,382 views; that is, this particular story was opened and read almost 2,400 times! President Bush's State of the Union address won't be read that many times online, so obviously there's something of importance to the waterfowling public here.

Perhaps the biggest question here, and I wish to get this out of the way so that we might move on to the more positive aspects of cyberspace as it relates to the waterfowler, is this: Is Internet scouting ethical, where Internet scouting is defined as viewing a photograph which has been voluntarily posted on a public forum, a.k.a. website, and subsequently using the information extracted from those observations to place yourself in the identical or an approximate location for the purpose of waterfowl hunting? Some would call such a tactic underhanded; others, myself included, feel that an entertaining and informative story can be told and photographs displayed publicly without revealing the whereabouts of the hunt, but that information made public goes into a well known as Public Information, and from this well, waterfowlers around the globe may draw. The bottom lines are these: If being scouted via Internet bothers you, don't post revealing photographs or text. If scouting via Internet post and photograph concerns you, don't do it. If you can sleep well after cross-referencing and researching a public image you've uncovered on the Internet, which leads you to a formerly unknown though public waterfowling location, so be it.

Look in his eyes. Are you really going to post pictures of the "secret" location that this young man took you to this morning on the net? Don't think so. PHOTO BY AVERY PRO-STAFF

Young Nick Miller can easily check the ebb and flow of the tides on the Columbia River, thanks to a number of different websites that feature such information.

ON TO THE GOOD

Regardless of how one personally feels about the topic of Internet scouting, it's difficult to argue with the fact that the primary purpose of the Internet is clear—the dissemination of information to the masses. Likewise, it's easy to see that the net does offer the waterfowler a vast pool of resources from which to draw. These resources, as I call them, are the C's:

Current and Constantly Updated Information

It's continually amazing to me just how much information is available via the net. True, there's a lot of separating the good from the bad—rather, the BS from the non-BS—that must go on as we decide that which we do and don't wish to distill from cyberspace, but this is an ability developed and honed with time.

One of the most positive attributes of the Internet, and one of particular importance to waterfowlers, is that the Information Superhighway spans the ages. The novice, the individual just breaking into waterfowling, who needs to know what and where and most importantly, how, can find an almost infinite amount of written and visual matter on the net. Chat rooms

When I hunted Mississippi with this gentleman, Mister Tommy Akin, our licenses were easily and conveniently purchased online prior to the trip.

and forums like those spotlighted below can be of great significance to the new guy in terms of developing a fundamental waterfowling education. A question is raised, and a thousand responses given; all the newcomer must do is read, and then ask questions of the responses. As for the field veteran, the net features electronic opportunities to advance through hunting's various stages, all with the click of a mouse.

Whether it's building your own layout boat, carving your first canvasback decoy, or doing the taxidermy on that beautiful drake harlequin, it's all there at your fingertips.

But it's the net's timeliness, the constant and continual revisions and updates, that attracts many waterfowlers to the realm of cyberspace. Today's weather right now, tomorrow's weather today—it's available immediately, and of major significance to, say, the traveling duck hunter. Migration reports, river levels, tide tables, even something as momentary as temporary road closures or detours can all be found, monitored and noted, thanks to the net.

Convenience

As a professional writer, I find the Internet, above all things, the epitome of convenience. As a waterfowler, too, I've discovered that bobbing and weaving through cyberspace can and does save me time and money. No

The Author's www. Picks

There are a million-plus waterfowl hunting-related websites already in existence, or so it seems, with many more joining the ranks every day. For example, a Google search for duck hunting turned up 1.86 million possibilities. Adding the word scouting to the mix narrowed the choices somewhat—only 492,000 there!—but still offered up a lifetime's worth of sifting through cyberspace.

That said, let me help you get started with an abridged list of some of my regular stops along the Information Highway. True, there's a lot more out there; however, these seem to offer precisely what I'm searching for in terms of pre-hunt data.

- Any of the state fish and wildlife websites—fantastic places to start—will provide the straight skinny on regulations, licenses, public lands, interoffice contacts such as wildlife area supervisors, waterfowl biologists, and refuge managers.
- The Duck Hunter's Refuge (duckhunter.net): A have-all waterfowl hunting website. Includes individual state forums and on-topic/off-topic sections such as decoy carving, taxidermy, and outdoor cooking. Note: As with any of the forum-based websites, the trick with the Refuge is to separate fact from fiction—and believe me, there's a lot of fiction there.
- Avery Outdoors (averyoutdoors.com): One of several manufacturer websites highlighting the company's products; however, Avery offers a waterfowl-based forum section featuring such topics as in-depth outdoor photography. The forum also offers the general waterfowling public—that is, you and me—the opportunity to "speak" with knowledgeable outdoor professionals like Fred Zink, Shawn Stahl, Field Hudnall, Chad Belding, and a long list of others.
- Waterfowler.com (waterfowler.com) and Duck Hunting Chat (duckhuntingchat.com): Similar in subject and scope to The Duck Hunter's Refuge mentioned earlier. Good places to compare notes and gather information, if you're willing and able to separate the proverbial wheat from the chaff; that is, true from false.
- The Mallard Club (themallardclub.net): Entertaining, but definitely not for young eyes. The Mallard Club is a no-holds-barred place populated by guys who know how to kill ducks, plain and simple; however, your 12-year-old might learn some things here that he shouldn't know until he's well into his 30s. Still, I find it a pseudo-welcome break from the "he's looking at me!" moderation on some of the other sites.
- Conservation organizations such as Ducks Unlimited (ducks.org) or Delta Waterfowl (deltawaterfowl.org): Really no explanation necessary here. Sure, you can join online, but you'll also find migration reports, waterfowl population updates, current events, outdoor news, and a wealth of how-to articles by some of the most recognized names in the industry. Definite bookmark material.
- For weather forecasts, go to the National Weather Service (nws.noaa.gov). Duck hunters live and breathe the weather, and the National Weather Service provides everything the waterfowler needs

longer do I have to (a) locate a registered license agent, (b) drive to said license agent's place of business, and (c) return home. All this now can be accomplished with a few clicks of the mouse and a credit card. Nonresident paperwork, too, is a breeze. While logged onto the particular state fish and wildlife agency's website, I can register to be notified of any and all noteworthy news releases and breaking information via e-mail; thus, I'm not only licensed, but constantly informed and updated. And after all, isn't scouting simply the accumulation of information?

Camaraderie

Over the past two decades, the net has grown into a virtual duck blind or goose pit, where individuals through word and visual image take others through the pre-season, the hunt, and the post-hunt remembrance and celebration. Wildlife managers share in

and more. By the day, the week, or the month—it doesn't matter. If it's weather, it's here.

- Refuge counts are offered by the Fish & Wildlife Service (fws.gov). They're called migratory waterfowl for a reason. So to keep track of the birds' movements as they hopscotch from one refuge to another down the line, the Fish & Wildlife Service's website is the go-to place. You might have to do a little electronic digging to find the place you're looking for, but it's there. Refuge counts, incidentally, are generally updated weekly.

- Check river levels at the U.S. Geological Survey website (waterdata.usgs.gov/nwis/rt). It's always a good thing to know not only what the Cache, Mississippi, Columbia, or Ohio is doing, but what it's *going* to do in terms of rise and fall in the future. This interactive state-by-state site allows the point-and-clicker access to info such as flood stage, crest, flow data, and more, all updated every 15 to 60 minutes (depending on the recording units and technology involved) and transferred to USGS offices across the country. I know this is a hunting book, but angler—this one's definitely for you.

- To check tide tables, go to saltwatertides.com. All right; so the guy in Iowa doesn't really give a hoot about the correlation between high tide and legal shooting time; however, the eider gunner in Maine or the bluebill shooter in Washington State does. To salt-gunners, tides are everything; and while I hope that this electronic version never replaces DOT's Tide Table book, it sure is convenient.

- Aerial photography, satellite imagery, topographical information is available at Google Earth (earth.

google.com), TerraServer (terraserver.com), and TopoZone (topozone.com). Maps aren't anything new to the waterfowling community. Spy-technology capable of pinpointing the whereabouts of individual ducks? Yeah, that's pretty new. Locating potential—that is, where the birds either are or might be—is a huge element within the whole that is scouting, and few tools are more valuable to he who seeks potential than a view from above. There may be something of a subscription cost involved with sites like TerraServer and others, but it's well worth the money.

The Internet's all about telling a story about the outdoor experience, but how much information is too much information?

these cyber-outings. So, too, do waterfowl biologists, field veterans, new guys, men, women, children, good hunters, and, well, some not-so-good hunters. The Internet, unmasked, is really just storytelling for the twenty-first century, complete with the same bonds and relationships that men initially made face to face, post-hunt, in a brew pub after the sun had faded and the shotguns had been cleaned and stacked away 'til morning next. Some men say little or nothing about where, speaking only of the hunt itself, of the experience. Others, fueled by the pint, ego, machismo, or any of a hundred individualized reasons, speak volumes—and then are slack-jawed when their formerly unoccupied slice of avian heaven has been trimmed into razor-thin portions. The net offers the modern waterfowler so incredibly much in terms of discovery; however, your pleasure or dissatisfaction depends entirely on what you put into it—or what you don't.

CHAPTER 8

Thirty-One Hardcore Waterfowl Strategies

THE SCENE: YOU'RE TWO-THIRDS OF THE way through the goose season, and you haven't been able to do a thing with your birds in a week. You've tried this, you've tried that, and nothing seems to work. What now?

The scene: The ducks are giving you the cold shoulder; they're not playing the game the way they should. Hell, you're running 48 magnum mallards and not one, but *two* spinners—just like everyone else, and the birds just aren't falling for it. You can't imagine that six widgeon decoys and a jerk cord would work . . . or would it? And coots?! You don't even own *a* coot decoy, let alone several coot decoys. Should you?

Today's waterfowl aren't the birds of twenty years ago. With technological innovations like anatomically perfect decoys, spinning wings, and guys capable of sounding more natural than the ducks or geese themselves—well, let's just say the flyways have become a whole different ballgame. No more paper plates for snows, recycled radials for Canadas, and misshapen *things* for mallards. Today's waterfowler is all about realism, both in sight and sound. It's about becoming invisible, and once things do happen, being able to capitalize on each gunning opportunity. It's about strategy, folks, and that what we have here—thirty-

This gentleman certainly is going the extra mile—in fact, up to his armpits—to put motion into his spread. What are you doing to up your chances for success? PHOTO BY AVERY PRO-STAFF

one down-and-dirty strategies that can put more birds in your face *and* at your feet.

1. Sleeping on the ice. With ice or snow on the ground, geese often land and immediately lay down; their body heat melts the hard cover, exposing the food beneath. With the food source uncovered, they'll feed, sleep, and loaf—all without rising. Sleeper or no leg decoys are very realistic under such conditions, and almost impossible for birds to ignore.

2. Patterning pays off in spades. Turkey hunters believe in patterning; why not waterfowlers? The first step in becoming a better shooter is knowing how your shotgun performs *each and every time* you pull the trigger. Time on the range before the opener with a variety of chokes and ammunition can make a huge difference.

3. Take a shooting lesson from a skilled instructor. We all shoot well enough, right? The truth is, most shotgunners—myself certainly included—could benefit from four to eight hours spent under the watchful eye of a trained shooting instructor. Lessons from the likes of Gil and Vicki Ash (www.ospschool.com), will take up where patterning and experimentation leave off.

*Left: No, sir. Things—decoys, guns, ammunition, and much more—are a lot different now than they were in 1972 when I killed my first duck. **Below:** Late season geese spend a lot of time on their bellies. Why shouldn't your decoys?*
BOTH PHOTOS BY AVERY PRO-STAFF

Above left: Turkey hunters do it all the time. Do you, Mister Waterfowler, bother to pattern your favorite fowling piece?
Above right: It's okay to be Type-A when it comes to concealment.

4. Rediscover pass-shooting. Pass-shooting can be productive, particularly during the late season. The key to successful pass-shooting is location; scouting before and during the season will give you the information you need regarding variables such as active flight lines and flight times. Then put yourself under the birds, and use restraint as to distance.

5. Concealment isn't a game. There's nothing wrong with being Type A about camouflage and concealment; hiding and becoming invisible is what it's all about. Cut enough brush for your blinds to last all season, and stack what you don't use some distance away. It will age with time, and will match the native vegetation perfectly when it's time to touch-up.

6. Pack a well-stocked blind bag. It's better to have it and not need it than need it and not have it. A properly outfitted blind bag has saved more than one hunt, with some of the bare essentials including cable ties, a cell phone, safety pins, vehicle lock de-icer, aspirin, Rolaids, emergency duct table, 20 feet of decoy cord, and—of course—toilet paper in a zipper-top bag 'cause socks ain't cheap.

7. Think small and out-of-the-way places. Is there a tiny, out-of-the-way corner of that pressured public

wetland that doesn't get much human attention? Detailed maps or websites such as terraserver.com or GoogleEarth.com can reveal the location of virtually untouched hunting hotspots—and if you're willing to walk and pack a small spread, you might be surprised.

8. Master the art of realism and natural movement. With today's decoys and birds as they are, modern spreads are all about realism and natural movement. Once you set your rig, step back and evaluate it. Does it look real? Does it move as it should? If it doesn't look natural to you, why should it look good to the ultimate judge backwinging overhead?

9. Discover the mystery of moving water. Moving water—tides, rivers, anything that flows—is, by virtue of that movement, more difficult to hunt than still waters; thus, they often don't see the hunting pressure received by impoundments, marshes, sheetwater, and the like. Find a quiet, shallow stretch of river, toss out a dozen water-keels mid-morning, and settle in.

10. Combine silhouettes with tradition. Have a stack of Canada silhouettes gathering dust in the corner? Get them out, get them clean, and mix them into a spread of full-bodies this fall. The appearing/disappearing that the two-dimensional cut-outs do gives the illusion of movement to birds in the air, and lends an event of realism to an otherwise frozen rig.

11. Try unique species in decoy spreads. Everyone runs Canadas for Canadas, and mallards for all ducks; why not give the birds something they *haven't* seen? Try six snows (the white really draws attention!) off to one side of your Canada spread. Or six drake sprig, widgeon, or grey ducks in your mallard rig. Maybe an all-widgeon spread? Often, different can be good.

Right: My theory is, 'tis better to have it and not need it than need it and not have it. That said, pack a good blind bag. Below: You don't need 100 acres to kill six ducks. Maybe that hidden quarter-acre pothole is the ticket. It's worth a look.

Myself, I like to mix up my spreads—specks or a couple snows with my Canadas; divers off to the side of a puddle duck rig. And then there's the all-coot spread. PHOTO BY AVERY PRO-STAFF

If you want something sure to be different than the guy down the way, make your own decoys.

12. Make your own decoys. As seen above, different can be good in terms of decoy spreads. And few spreads are as unique as those which are hand-made. In addition to presenting a visual that's altogether new, even to stale birds, hand-carved and painted decoys are often a source of pride for their creator—not to mention helping speed the off-season days.

13. Learn a second language. Mallard hen quacks work fine in many cases, but what about when it doesn't? The nasally dweek of a drake mallard, the dink . . .

Left: Okay, so it's technically a hawk call; however, with it, I can speak teal, drake mallard, pintail, and widgeon—oh, and red-tailed hawk too. **Below:** *The more you learn about ducks and geese, the better able you'll be to answer your own questions. Never stop studying the real thing.* PHOTO BY AVERY PRO-STAFF

Complete concealment, attention to detail, proper decoy placement, noise discipline—all elements in the equation known as efficiency. PHOTO BY AVERY PRO-STAFF

dink-dink of a grey duck, or the breathy whistle of a baldpate, combined with the traditional quacks and rolling chuckles, can be music to even the most jaded duck's ears.

14. Go back to school. Today's duck and goose gurus are some of the best in history. And what's more, they're accessible to us—the common guys. Thanks to the Internet, outdoors educators like Fred Zink, Field Hudnall, and Tim Grounds are right at our fingertips. So go ahead. Ask questions. Read the forums. Study the DVDs. And practice.

15. Teach your decoys to swim. When river hunting, modify three or four decoys as such: About three inches back from the traditional anchor point, drill a hole through the keel (water-keel), or press a red-hot fence staple into the plastic (weighted-keel); tie your cord here. The leading edge works like a crankbait lip, causing the decoy to *swim* back and forth in the current.

16. Study, study, study what makes real birds real. Pros like Allan Stanley or Scott Threinen are good at what they do because they never stop studying their subjects; in these boys' case, geese. Watching and listening to birds year-round can greatly increase your knowledge base when it comes time to set the decoys and blinds.

17. Pay strict attention to detail. I'll make this one easy. There is no such thing as an insignificant detail when it comes to hiding from or attracting via decoy ducks and geese. Sure, sloppy hunters kill some birds. But sloppy hunters aren't consistent hunters, and consistency means paying attention to *all* the details. Make it look good, and keep it looking good.

18. Create on-the-water motion. Spinning wing decoys and other gadgetry may be all the rage now, but it's hard to beat a good, old-fashioned jerk cord for (a) creating the illusion of motion, and (b) attracting ducks. Use a lightweight water-keel decoy; they *bounce* better and send out more ripples. And when in doubt, drop the call and pull the string.

19. Strive for efficiency. As the season progresses, take a minute to evaluate the efficiency of your rig. Can you pick up and move quickly, if need be? Is your spread easy to handle? Does your blind function flawlessly? Is your boat blind organized? Being efficient in the field drastically reduces wasted time and energy—energy that could be spent working birds.

20. Get a small boat. Small skiffs like the Aqua-pod, Momarsh Fat Boy, or Carstens Puddler, simply put, can get you into places where others can't go. Such boats are lightweight, very mobile, and can be

launched damn near anywhere. They also double as blinds and pack vehicles, taking you and your rig to those unpressured out-of-the-way places.

21. Back away from your blocks. When late-season geese get decoy-wise, try this: Set six or eight full-bodies in the open where there's goose traffic; say, a cut beanfield. Use natural cover—a fencerow or brushpile—as a blind 60 to 80 yards downwind. As the birds check the decoys but *before* they slide off, they should be in range.

22. Add coots to your arsenal. An all-coot spread can be very effective, particularly for pressured birds.

The trick is motion. Set twenty to twenty-five coots in a blob; it doesn't matter if they're touching. Rig a jerk cord with four to six coots, and put it center mass of the spread. The goal is to create a feeding frenzy—it works incredibly well on widgeon.

23. Upgrade your present decoy spread. Natural-looking, realistic decoys are productive decoys. Take the time to not only keep your blocks clean—cold water and a stiff-bristled brush only; no soap as it can enhance ultra-violet sheen—but to paint and upgrade as needed. Flocked goose decoys are very lifelike, and a fresh coat of colors will do wonders for a mallard spread.

Left: It's all about "strag-a-tee," as old Mister Bugs Bunny was fond of saying. And that screwy rabbit wasn't too far wrong. PHOTO BY AVERY PRO-STAFF *Above: Four decoys just might work better than forty, especially if everyone and his brother is spreading forty. Don't be afraid to do something different.*

24. Downsizing works. On pressured or late-season birds, small spreads—eight Canada decoys, or ten mallards with a jerk cord—often produce better, simply because they're different from everything the birds are seeing. Realize, though, low numbers mean the utmost in realism—use the best you can afford, and keep them up to spec.

25. Never hesitate to move. Being mobile is but one aspect of successful waterfowling; actually moving when you need to is a whole 'nother story. Yes, it's often inconvenient to pack up and relocate, sometimes only two or three hundred yards away, but it's also frustrating to sit and watch birds work where you *could be*. If you can, move.

26. Go *au natural*. No, it's not what you might be thinking. Blinds are nice, sure, but sometimes the best blind is what Mother Nature provides—the edge of a cornfield, a fenceline, or a small stand of cattails. In the past, donning dark camo and becoming a rock at the water or tideline has provided some exceptional gunning.

27. Hunt the mid-morning flight. In Washington, we had a 9 A.M. flight; in Iowa, it's 10 o'clock. Either way, it's not to be missed—and often, Maggie, my black Lab, and I are the only hunters around to reap the benefits of hunting the mid-morning shift. Watch the weather, and learn your birds—you might not have to get up at 3:30 anymore.

28. Hunt with and learn from the best. Curb your ego and open your mind. There's a lot of information out there from knowledgeable waterfowlers across the

country; take advantage of it. I've learned volumes over the past twenty years from hunters, young and old. Everyone has a trick up their sleeve, and most are willing to share.

29. Take a trip. Start saving money now, and once a year, take a trip. It doesn't have to be far, and it needn't be expensive—what it will be is a break from the routine. From here in eastern Iowa, it might be a layout hunt on the Mississippi, a week freelancing in South Dakota, or a no-holds-barred adventure to Saskatchewan. Regardless, treat yourself.

30. Suck it up. Unless you're constantly grinding 'fowl for pepperoni, long-term storage of ducks and geese can be an issue; however, the modern vacuum packer can prove a first-rate, affordable solution. A couple goose fillets or a half-dozen mallards, vacuum-sealed, will last a year or longer in the ice-chest with no sign of freezer burn.

Left: Start saving now and take a trip to Maine for eiders. Or Washington for harlequins. Or coastal Texas for redheads. Below: If the birds tell you to move, move. Just put it on your back, pick 'em up, and do it. PHOTO BY AVERY PRO-STAFF

Above: And here it is: the big pay-off. Are you to this point? Right: A vacuum packer will save you hundreds of dollars in short order in terms of wild game not wasted due to freezer burn.

31. The big pay-off. When you've done everything right and left nothing to chance, these are the kinds of images that will be indelibly etched onto your gray matter, as well they should. The best waterfowlers don't depend on luck to fill their game straps. They're good at what they do because they practice and they're persistent—as, too, you should be.

CHAPTER 9

ABCs of
Goose Hunting

"IT'S NOT ROCKET SCIENCE." I CAN'T TELL YOU how many times I've heard calling legend, Buck Gardner, say that when someone claims to be having trouble with a duck call. Well, folks, the same rocket science principle applies to goose hunting. If you learn the basic steps—the ABCs, we'll call them here—you can apply those tactics and lessons all season long, while at the same time growing more confident in your abilities and more effective as a waterfowler.

That said, we'd like to present Goose Hunting's ABCs:

A. Ammunition: An elemental consideration, yes, but vital nonetheless. Choose carefully. I prefer Hevi-Shot #2s in a 3-inch 12-gauge as a do-all load, the same in #4s over decoys or BBs when distances grow a bit. Pre-season patterning with various choke and load combinations is a must.

B. Blinds: I can't stress enough the importance of these three words—attention to detail—when it comes to hiding and staying hidden. Remember, blinds should conceal the shooter; you're not trying to conceal the blind. That is, don't use so much of anything as to be unnatural.

C. Calling: Practice and self-confidence are two vital keys to goose calling success. Find one call that

*As this big Iowa honker is about to discover, it's not all rocket science—
it's all about being prepared.* PHOTO BY AVERY PRO-STAFF

Above: Your choice in terms of ammunition can make or break a hunt. Choose wisely, and then pattern and practice. Right: Minnesotan Scott Threinen uses a fenceline for a blind and a small, easy-to-manage spread during the early September season. PHOTO BY AVERY PRO-STAFF

you're comfortable with, and then learn to blow it. Many instructional tools exist—cassettes, educational DVDs, calling seminars, or even one-on-one tutorials with the call-makers themselves.

D. Decoys: Keep 'em clean, and watch the geese in your area. Those live birds will tell you how many decoys to use, and how to set them once you're afield. Get the highest quality decoys your wallet will allow. And don't feel like you have to use them all; sometimes, fewer is better.

E. Early season: During the September early season, Minnesotan and competitive caller Scott Threinen tries not to show the local birds everything he has in his goose-hunting arsenal. "You have to save something for later in the season," says Threinen. "For when the birds get tough."

F. Flagging: Just ask The Flagman, Randy Bartz, and he'll tell you that there's a hell of a lot more to effective flagging than simply waving a black rag around. A common mistake guys make, says Bartz, is stopping too soon. You have the birds' attention—then nothing. Often, the time to stop flagging is when you grab your shotgun.

G. Grounds, Tim: I hope I don't embarrass him when I refer to Timmy Grounds as The Godfather of Goose. And if I do, the fact remains that his is one

of the names to be indelibly etched on the walls of the Goose Hunting Hall of Fame when they knock down that building in Cleveland and build a *good* museum.

H. Hudnall, Field: This young Kentuckian turned Buckeye Stater has more goose calling championships under his belt than Carter has little liver pills—and that's a bunch. You can watch Field at work in the latest Zink Calls DVD, *Runnin' Traffic.* It's an educational experience, trust me.

I. Invisible: Whether you're in a pit, a Finisher, or hunkered in the horse weeds, it doesn't matter; what matters is that you're invisible to the birds overhead. This means your personal camouflage works, your blind matches the surroundings, and you know how to stay still.

J. Junkyard spread: An arrangement of goose decoys consisting of every type and style imaginable, including silhouettes, shells, full-bodies, inflatables, wigglers, shakers, spinners, kites, the kitchen sink, and an old cardboard box. If you can, stick with one style; numbers don't always matter.

K. Kluck: I know; it's spelled wrong, but I wanted to work this one in somewhere. The cluck is the yelp or the grunt in the goose hunter's vocabulary. As calling great Shawn Stahl says, "It's a honk, but it's a very short honk." It's important you learn this one first.

What's he saying? Can you understand him? Better yet, can you speak his language? Best be learning. PHOTO BY AVERY PRO-STAFF

You can't just shake the Black Rag around and expect it to work. The Flagman says there's a trick to it—best listen. PHOTO BY AVERY PRO-STAFF

Make your blinds invisible, and you'll kill more birds. It's that simple.

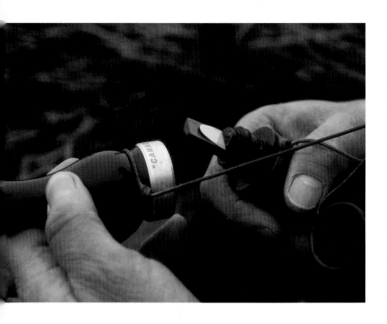

Above: Reeds needn't be mysterious objects. However, if you aren't efficient with the call, do not attempt to modify the reed; that is, unless you have another $200 you're willing to part with. Right: Curt Wilson will answer your questions about goose hunting; all you have to do is ask.

L. Low-profile blinds: These modern day conglomerations of cordura nylon and aircraft aluminum are the above-ground equivalent of the traditional pit blind. They're lightweight, easily camouflaged, and as the name implies, extremely low-profile. More than two dozen versions exist today.

M. Motion: Just as in a duck spread on the water, motion in a dry-land goose rig is important in order to achieve realism. Flagging works well; so, too, do decoy-and-stake combinations (i.e. Greenhead Gear's RealMotion Field Stakes) that allow lightweight decoys to virtually walk through a spread.

N. Non-steel: I'm a huge fan of the non-steel non-toxic shotshells that are available to today's 'fowler, particularly those geared toward big game like geese. Hevi-Shot's offerings are tremendous, as are other exotics such as Winchester's Extended Range and Federal's High Density.

O. OLT A-50: A traditional flute style goose call. Shawn Stahl says, "It's the standard, the one that most of the flute calls on the market today are designed after." I have a Mike Weller-modified A-50, and absolutely love it. Plus, flutes are different from the barrage of short-reeds that geese hear; think about it.

P. Patterning: Turkey hunters are *huge* on patterning; why, then, aren't waterfowlers as tuned into this oh-so-important aspect of the shotgunning process? Patterning simply takes time, but it's time well spent. There's no sense in achieving perfection if your pattern isn't perfect.

Q. Questions: I realize it's unmanly to ask questions and directions; still, there are thousands of experienced goose hunters out there who would be more than happy to help solve your gunning dilemmas. Check out websites like averyoutdoors.com or flocknocker.com

R. Reed: In layman's terms, it's the little white thing inside the goose call that moves up and down when you blow through it, thus making a noise that—hopefully—sounds like a goose. Commonly made from Mylar (plastic), reeds can be trimmed, shaved or otherwise altered to change the tone of the call.

S. Scouting: Ask any 100 avid goose hunters, and 100 of them will say that scouting is, without question, the key element to in-the-field success. Find your birds, and then observe them—how many there are, what time they leave and arrive, how they are arranged on the ground, and more.

T. Tuning: Tuning is, as Stahl defines, "the art of adjusting or modifying the reed and reed assembly of a goose call" in order to modify the sound, specifically the tone or pitch, emanating from said call. The rule of thumb is: If you can't blow it, don't tune it.

U. Understanding: The more you know—that is, understand—about geese, their biology, and their daily habits, the better armed you'll be when you head out to scout. You'll know to look for variables like flock size, flock distribution, preferred food sources, and other factors.

V. Volume: The first geese of the morning will tell you exactly how you have to call that day, including the volume needed to get those birds to do what you want them to do. Not all goose calling is loud calling; often, the subtle stuff—the clucks, moans, and murmurs— will seal the deal.

Left: Plain and simple, scouting is the key to successful goose hunting. Play it down, and you take your chances. **Above, top:** The very best goose hunters hunt geese year-round. They watch, listen, take photographs . . . and they learn. PHOTO BY JOE FLADELAND **Above, bottom:** Not all goose calling is loud calling. Aural modulation is an important aspect of effective calling.

Above: Freddie Zink, here in Canada, understands Elements A through Y—and that's why he's good at what he does, and that's hunt geese. **Right:** *Notice all the snow goose heads? It's all about wind direction—and if it changes, you must as well.* PHOTO BY AVERY PRO-STAFF

W. Wind direction: How you arrange your decoy spread and where you position your blinds in relation to that spread depends almost entirely on wind direction. Wind speed, too, is vital; too much, and the birds hover to pick you apart. Too little, and they can land anywhere . . . if they land at all.

X. X marks the spot: Being on the X, the very spot where the birds were in the field as determined by your scouting, is definitely a plus; however, it doesn't guarantee a good shoot. And for those not on the X, aggressive calling, a realistic spread, and some flagging can make all the difference.

Y. Year-round: The best goose hunters *hunt* geese year-round; that is, they harvest birds during the season, and then study their quarry for the remaining nine months. These hardcore carve decoys, shoot photography, or even catch live birds on video—all in the name of furthering their education.

Z. Zink, Fred: A former champion competitive caller turned call-maker, decoy carver, and R & D man for Avery Outdoors, Ohioan Freddie Zink studies Canada geese 365 days a year—and that's what makes him the very best at what he knows . . . geese.

CHAPTER 10

Rails and Snipe: A Marshland Tradition

I'LL NEVER FORGET MY FIRST RAIL HUNT.
Rather, I'll never forget the one thought that ran
through my then 23-year-old head throughout the
whole of my first rail hunt. That thought? Why would
three supposedly sane men, each armed with hundreds
of dollars worth of shotguns and ammunition, take
a reasonably well-adjusted yellow Lab dog and wade
through the September swamp, all the while searching
for a bird no larger than a sparrow and just slightly
more capable of flight than, say, a Pop Tart?

Well, the truth of the whole matter is that it took
all of that inaugural rail hunt in order for me to arrive
at an answer. Fact is, it required a subsequent hunt,
perhaps two, before I realized just why these three
men and their yellow dog would do something like
this. It's fun. That's all there is to it. It's just plain fun.

Rail hunting, at least the rail hunting that I've been
exposed to, is the epitome of elementalism. You don't
need fancy guns. And you don't need fancy clothes.
Truth is, the uniform of many a midwestern rail hunter
consists only of a tattered pair of 25-cent garage sale
blue jeans, an equally familiarized t-shirt, and an old
pair of Chuck Taylor high-top tennis shoes. You know,
the ones with the little rubberized circle on the ankle

With no dove season, September in Iowa—at least for Jet and me—is all about hunting rails.

bones and the metal-rimmed holes in the sides? Those holes are important to the rail hunter as the pair on the left side let the water in while the ones on the right let the swamp water out. If you didn't have that second set of holes, well . . . we'll get to rail clothing here in bit.

Some, if not many of you at this point, are scratching your head, or some other unmentionable yet favorite portion of your anatomy, and asking no one in particular a very justifiable question: Just what the hell is a rail? Well, this seems like the perfect segue into a portion of these chapters which I'm fond of calling:

MEET THE PLAYERS

Believe it or not, North America is home to not one or two, but four species of rails. These include the Virginia, sora, clapper, and king rails. Personally, I've

hunted only the smaller sora; however, I have seen numbers of clapper rails while cast-netting shrimp on North Carolina's Intercoastal Waterway, and have always wanted to return to these saltwater marshes during the fall of the year to take part in what the locals speak of as a most traditional yet today seldom seen hunting opportunity.

As a group, the rails are relatively small and secretive—though at times quite noisy—birds. Each makes its home among the reeds and cattails of the country's marshes—some on the coasts, and others scattered throughout the remainder of the Lower 48. A closer look at these interesting game birds provides the up-and-coming rail hunter with a bit of pre-outing background, not to mention some valuable clues to the question, Which one is that?

The Virginia rail: Like all rails, the Virginia rail is, well, brown. And small. Small as in an average weight of only five ounces. And small as in an overall size of roughly 10 inches from beak tip to tail feathers. What there are of them. And again like all rails, the Virginia sports long, gangly legs that dangle below the bird during those infrequent occasions when you're successful in getting your quarry to actually leave the comfort of the marsh grass. All this said, though, the Virginia rail is in fact the country's most familiar member of the family, with populations of one kind or another inhabiting all of the Lower 48 and portions of southern Canada. Freshwater marshes are the Virginia's habitat of choice; however, freeze-up will see a migration, be it brief or lengthy, onto coastal saltwater environments.

The sora rail: As I mentioned earlier, the sora is the species that I'm familiar with, and the one that I reintroduce myself to each September. To tell you the truth, I've grown quite fond of this odd little bird with the lima bean–colored legs and the frustrating habit of flying no higher than $3^{1}/_{2}$ feet—and slowly at that—before falling back into the tules. At 23, I was quick enough on the draw to shoot at those rails. At 38, I need a good 12 feet before I can even find the fore-end of the over-under. But I digress. . . . In size, the sora rail is comparable to a small robin, minus the tail. The overall coloration is a slate gray, although the back and wings are a mixture of muted browns and blacks, some

In a good stiff wind, rails can actually get up a little speed. Doves, they're not, but challenging given the right day.

My Rail Mentor

Whenever I tell someone that I hunt rails, there is this pause while they wait for a punch line that never comes. I know they're thinking that it's a setup similar to the old snipe-hunting prank that involved a burlap bag and a flashlight. Maybe most are disappointed that the joke never came, but a few have actually followed up on an invitation to hunt. Mike Johnson was one of the few who took a chance and now knows that rails really do exist and that hunting them is just about the most fun a bird hunter can have in September.

We hunted a large public marsh where I often had the entire area to myself. I had a yellow Lab who got pretty good at figuring out the tactics necessary to putting these secretive birds to flight, and he got very good at recovering birds that had fallen into the spaces between cattails and rice cut grass. The dog and I learned rail hunting together and for a couple of years we had a ball. He would come home with his brown nose all cut up from the sharp edges of the grass we had to push through, and I would come home with socks so black from marsh mud that I just threw them out.

Now most people couldn't identify a rail if one landed on their head. This of course adds to the mystique and I'm sure is one of the main reasons that I've had so much good ground all to myself. Acres of cattails, spatterdock, rice cut grass, and smartweed harbored enough birds to keep us interested for a month. When we found birds, the action was fast, the shooting a challenge, and the retrieves were fascinating. Rails hate to fly and know as many tricks to avoid man and dog as two-year-old Iowa pheasant. Major and I sort of figured these things out together, as you will, I suspect.

Now maybe you'll try your hand at rail hunting and maybe you won't. All I expect is that the next time you pass a marsh when the cattails are just starting to turn brown that you'll wonder about those mysterious little birds. Rails are no joke. They are real. Real fun.

—Mike Moutoux, Education Officer for the
 Ohio Department of Natural Resources,
 Division of Wildlife, and the individual
 solely responsible for introducing me to
 the enjoyment that is rail hunting

---

edged in white. The legs, as said, are a light green, while the short yet stout-looking beak is a soft lemon yellow. Who would the sora rail look like if it were a famous person? Maybe—and forgive me—Lou Costello. With a short neck, chunky body, yellow nose, and green legs. As for flight and flight speed, I'm sorry; you pheasant and grouse hunters are going to be sorely disappointed, not only with the sora, but the Virginia and the clapper as well. Rails as a group would much rather run from danger than fly; however, when forced into the air, rails move with all the grace, speed, and agility of a broken lawn chair pushed from the loading door of an out-of-service C-130. But, I have had hunts, all under very windy conditions, when the local sora population flew as well as any snipe or woodcock. Now that was challenging. Like its cousin, the Virginia rail, the sora prefers freshwater haunts, only heading toward the salt when the weather dictates. Here in Iowa, and in Ohio where I was first introduced

to the sora, I've always found the birds in good numbers in the same marshes where I would hunt teal later in the month of September.

The clapper rail: Larger than either the Virginia or sora, the clapper rail can be compared, size-wise, to that ubiquitous marsh dweller, the American coot, a.k.a. the mud hen, weighing in at slightly under one pound and measuring some 14 to 16 inches from stem to stern. Body coloration is a light gray. Long, pale legs and a two-inch-long beak, a probing tool used to procure the clapper's favored foods of shrimp, small crabs, and tiny fish, round out the bird's somewhat odd appearance. Midwesterners such as myself seldom see clapper rails, the birds being inhabitants of coastal salt marshes.

The king rail: I turned on the television the other day just in time to catch the beginning of a North Carolina hunt for, of all things, rails. Using small wooden skiffs, one hunter would pole or push the craft through the salt marsh vegetation while the shooter,

September in the Midwest means heat, and the water's nice for man and dog alike.

side-by-side at the ready, would stand in the bow and tend to the responsibility of ammunition expenditure. What was surprising to me, particularly since the quarry were rails, was (1) how much more strong and agile these birds seemed on the wing, and (2) how often the shooter missed. Twice. Still, the tradition that is East Coast rail hunting was definitely there, and the men constantly discussed the fact that few if any folks took the time to pole the salt marshes today in search of what these gentleman obviously considered the king of upland game birds, the king rail. As befitting the name, the king rail is the largest of the North American rails, often weighing 18 to 20 ounces, and stretching some 20 inches in length. A plain brown is the overall color, broken only by lighter streaking and mottling. The long (3 to 3$^1/_2$ inches) yellowish bill is tipped in black. Freshwater marshes, while open, are the king's preferred bailiwick; however, the species can be found sharing the company of the saltwater-loving clapper rail once Mother Nature says it's time for a calendar-related change of venue.

THE SEASON OF THE RAIL

Across most of the country, rail season begins in early September and continues through mid-November, give or take a few days. Understand, please, that those in the northern states will both begin and end their annual season a bit earlier, while hunters residing below the Mason-Dixon line will open and close a bit later.

For me, rail season has always meant September. In most cases, this early opener provides me with my first wingshooting opportunity of the year, thanks in large part to Governor Tom Vilsack and his veto of Iowa's latest dove hunting legislation. Appreciate it, Tom. A September rail season also provides me and my black Labs with some much-needed physical exercise, something I haven't had since the close of turkey season, and conditioning that helps prepare me for the more rigorous waterfowl, deer, and fall turkey outings on the horizon.

Come mid-October, though, most rail hunting in the Midwest is all but over. Many hunters, myself included, have set their sights on other game. And a large percentage of the birds themselves have moved along, pushed toward southern climes by the first of Mother Nature's wintry winds. Now's the time that the traditionalists living in the Virginias and the Carolinas emerge, side-by-sides in hand, to dust off the small skiffs and look out over the salt marshes, a cupped hand to one ear, listening for the unseen rustlings and B-movie chatterings that mean but one thing—it's rail time again.

RAIL GUNS AND AMMUNITION

If you've read our previous books, or if you've but read this far in this particular project, you will know by now that I'm what I'll refer to as an elementalist when it comes to hunting. Some folks, my wife in particular, prefer to use the word simple instead of elementalist. Either way, my point is this—I enjoy the no-frills aspect that comes with certain types of hunting. Jump-shooting, for instance. Or an evening spent looking over four hand-me-down decoys with a black Lab named Maggie at your side. Maybe it's heading into the uplands armed with your Grandma's Savage .410 single shot and four shotshells. Remember now, the limit on roosters is three. Or it's a morning rail hunt. Now there's simple, and that's one of the reasons, if not *the* reason, that I thoroughly enjoy rail hunting. There are no Robo-Rails, and should someone make one in the coming year, I will not buy it. There are no rail decoys, although there used to be snipe decoys and from what I understand, the old-timers said they worked rather well at times; however, I'm getting ahead of my species here. Rail hunting doesn't require dry-clean-only clothing nor shotguns whose price tags approximate double house payments. There's really no scouting, no maps, and no global positioning systems needed to be a successful rail hunter.

So, that all said, what do you need? Certainly first to be considered is the gun. And immediately, a question comes to mind. Does there exist the perfect rail gun? And my answer to that is a resounding no, and who cares. My first steps as an up-and-coming railman saw me toting a Remington 11-87 12-gauge. Since then, however, I've learned that where rails and guns are concerned, two very simple terms apply—light and

One of the best rail guns I've ever carried—a Browning Citori Lightning Feather in 20-gauge.

small. There's no sense in packing a 9-pound shotgun through the tules when a 5.5-pound over/under provides more than enough firepower for even the most aggressive sora or clapper. And there's no reason for a 28-inch barrel when a 21- or 24-inch tube will do just fine; however, if a 28-inch is what you have, then a 28-inch will work as well as any.

During the course of the fourteen years that I've chased rails, I've talked with hunters who have used scatterguns ranging from .410s to 12s, and everything in between. Myself? I carry one of two pieces into the September marsh—a Remington 870 Youth Model 20-gauge with a 21-inch barrel, cylinder choke tube, and a traditional 14.5-inch stock, the latter my only modification to this particular piece. My second rail gun of choice is a newly acquired Browning Citori Lightning Feather 20-gauge over/under choked Modified and Full. Both guns weigh next to nothing, and provide everything I need. They're a joy to carry, simple to clean, and, from a psychological standpoint,

It's a bit heavy and a little too much gun for rails; still,
my Remington M11–87 12-gauge performs well.

don't make me feel as though I've wheeled a 105mm field artillery piece into the swamp in search of sparrows. Even the playing field, so to speak.

Next is ammunition. And again, those two words come into play—light and small. Oh, and non-toxic. Yes, it's true. Because rails, and snipe as well, are migratory game birds, non-toxic shotshells are mandatory. Unfortunately, this switch from lead to non-toxics has cost the sport some in the way of participation; however, and fortunately, there are modern non-toxics, and by non-toxics I'm talking steel, that are not only much better performance-wise than the original loads, but fall into that pleasant category known as affordable.

So, with that said, our attention turns to specifics. In my 20-gauge guns, my choice of rail fodder runs to Winchester's light steel loads in 2.75-inch containing ³/4 ounce of #7 shot. Thrown from a Cylinder or Improved bore, this particular round gives me everything I need, both for the frequent at-arms-length flushes as well as those occasional wild rises. Too, I'm a big fan of this round for its use on the snipe fields, which frequently adjoin the marshes that rails call home. If you choose to shoot a 12-gauge, Winchester also supplies a light 12 load, also in steel #7, as do the folks at Remington Arms; however, for those of you looking for something non-toxic and non-steel, Remington offers their new Hevi-Shot shotshells in a rail and snipe-perfect 2.75-inch 12-gauge hull filled with #9 shot. A bit more expensive? Yes. Actually, a lot more expensive; still, if you're looking for something that will serve double-duty on snipe, rails, and the occasional loafing blue-wing teal or woodie that you're fortunate enough to sneak on during the latter days of September, it's tough to beat the lead-like qualities of Hevi-Shot.

No, I haven't forgotten those of you who might wish to carry that nostalgic .410, 28, or 16-gauge into the rail marsh. There's non-toxic ammunition for you folks too; however, you're going to have to contact the good people at the Bismuth Cartridge Company for your rail hunting shotshell needs, especially if it's the smaller (#7.5 through #9) shot sizes that you're looking for. True, both Remington and Federal offer a 16-gauge non-toxic load; however, you're limited there to a choice between #2 steel and #4 steel, both of which are, in my opinion, a bit on the huge size for something like rails.

Maggie and me with a partial limit of rails. Ammunition of choice here were light (1-ounce) steel No. 7s.

DRESSING FOR RAIL SUCCESS

I think I'm pretty safe in saying that damn little has been written about the right and wrong way to dress for the purposes of hunting rails. And while I, as I mentioned, have hunted the birds for nigh on fifteen years, I'm sure there are things that I don't know in terms of clothing and the art of rail hunting; however, the one thing that I do know is this. Unless you're into pain and personal suffering, *do not under any circumstances* hunt rails in shorts. No, this rule doesn't apply to you push-polers on the salt marshes. The folks I'm

talking to are the folks like me, the ones who wade into the water and the tules and the lily pads and the muskrat houses into search of their birds. Just let me put it this way. Sawgrass? Well, it's named sawgrass for a reason. 'Nough said.

Okay, so if you don't wear shorts, what do you wear? Well, remember what I said back in the beginning of this chapter? That thing about the 25-cent blue jeans, old t-shirt, and holey tennis shoes? I was serious. If it could be called an ensemble, that would be my rail hunting ensemble. The tennis shoes protect my feet, the jeans protect my legs, and the shirt serves as a barrier between me, the sun, and the 1.462 million mosquitoes who look upon my as a walking version of a Big Mac. Oh, and a hat. But that's really all there is to rail hunting and clothes. No camouflage necessary.

Left: Jet prefers a red collar and a sprinkling of duck weed as part of her rail ensemble; I'm prone to jeans and a t-shirt.
Below: This light strap-style vest lets me carry water, ammunition, snacks, and—hopefully—a limit (12 in Iowa) of rails.

Here, hunting partner, Phil Bourjaily, uses his blaze orange cap as a marker while searching for a downed sora rail.

Besides, who ever heard of hiding from a rail? The next thing you know, we'll be building rail blinds.

Sometimes, on occasion, I will don a pair of light (key word: light) chest waders prior to leaving terra firma. Lightweight chest waders not only keep me dry, but they also help protect from cuts, abrasions, and the inevitable bugs. My advice on hip boots? Yes, at first, hip boots might seem a wise choice, due to the heat and all, but hip boots also have an irritating habit of transforming themselves into thigh-high collectors of all sorts of foreign objects, including but not limited to seed heads, cattail fuzz, bugs, small mammals, and those black-and-yellow banana spiders, just the thought of which will keep me out of even the most pristine rail marsh.

Accessorizing? Not much at all; however, there are a couple items that might make your rail hunting experience a bit more enjoyable. These include:

- A light hunting vest with a game bag, for obvious reasons. Or, if you'd like to get specific, for your bullets and your bagged rails.
- Insect repellent. Again, the reason is painfully obvious. One word about insect repellents. Watch those with high concentrations of DEET. It's a wonderful thing for keeping the bugs away, but it can always wreck havoc with gun finishes. Perhaps a better choice for you and your gun might be something like Avon's Skin-So-Soft with Bug Guard. And who cares if you smell nice. These aren't whitetails.
- A small water bottle 'cause rail hunting is hard, thirsty work.
- A yellow hankie weighted at one corner with a lead fishing sinker. Small and brown, rails can be notoriously difficult to find once downed. Enter the hankie. Keep it in your back pocket, just like a football referee would. When you drop a bird, grab the hankie and toss it in the direction the bird fell. The sinker? It gives the rag distance and, for lack of a better phrase, flight stability. And another thing. Always mark your birds down well, and never take your eye off that spot until you've thoroughly searched.
- And finally, your retriever. That is, if you have one. Our black Labs, Maggie and Jet, dearly love to hunt anything, including rails. Truth is, they both have been very instrumental in helping me locate birds that have fallen in heavy cover or those that I hadn't marked properly. Too, a pair of slightly overweight Labs thrashing around in the tules has a way of unnerving even the most cagy sora rail and forcing it into the air. Sure, he'll land four feet away and run off, but at least I saw him, eh?

I'VE GOT ONE, NOW WHAT?

A good question. And the answer, not surprisingly, is just as elemental—clean it, cook it, and eat it.

Cleaning a rail, be it sora or king, is really no different than cleaning a dove. Most certainly, you can pluck the bird whole, if you choose. And some folks, myself on occasion, do this. Commonly, however, rails are cleaned simply by breasting the bird. This can be accomplished using one's thumb and a quick flick of the wrist, or with a pair of game shears. A quick rinse, and the entire process shouldn't have required more than half a minute.

Next, the cooking process. Mike Moutoux, when he was rail hunting, had a recipe for what he called Rail Nuggets. Mike actually filleted the breast halves off the bone, dipped them in a milk-and-egg mixture, rolled them in seasoned flour, and deep-fat fried them. Done as such, I liked them. Small, they were, but actually quite good. A little like gizzards. Myself, I flour the entire breast, brown it in a skillet, and put a couple dozen of them (I put on one major Rail Feed each year!) into a small crock-pot with a little orange juice, red wine, garlic oil, and a can of cream of mushroom soup. This I'll serve over rice to anyone who's around. Fellow writer Phil Bourjaily plucks his rails whole, splits them up the back, seasons them with a little salt and pepper, and plops them on the grill. Or—and this is about as complicated a rail recipe as I've ever heard—again from Bourjaily, he'll breast the birds, quick-sear them in a frying pan, wrap breast now housing a slice of water chestnut in fat bacon, and grill the whole thing, skewered, on the barbeque. I'll substitute the water chestnut for a hunk of jalapeño pepper, but I'll certainly give it a try. As should you.

Ah, and now the $64,000 question: So, just what do rails taste like? Well, they don't taste like chicken.

SNIPE DEFINED

All stories aside (see sidebar), snipe are indeed real things. Like rails, these evolved shorebirds, also known formally as Wilson's snipe and informally as jacksnipe, are small, with most weighing from five to seven ounces and measuring only a foot or so from tip to tail. And three inches of that tip is beak—a very

Think doves are challenging on the wing? Try a snipe before he settles down and flies straight. Humbling, it is.

distinctive, woodcock-esque light-colored bill that the snipe uses as a probing tool as it searches for insects, worms, aquatic bugs, snails, and other creepy-crawlers.

Perhaps surprisingly, snipe are a plain-pretty kind of creature, what with their streaks of brown and buff interrupted by white. For the most part, the bird's underparts are a mottled white, while the back contains an assortment of darker hues. The tail, again like the woodcock, is short and stubby, with a rusty-reddish tinge; the legs, like the sora rail's, a light greenish. The bottom line? My guess is that somewhere down the line, a dowitcher, or perhaps a plover or yellowlegs, crossed paths with a woodcock, with the result of the subsequent courtship and mingling—yep, you guessed it, a snipe. Probably not true, but it sounds good.

A bird of the wetlands, snipe can often be found in the company of rails. Or at least in the same general area, with, that is, one exception. Whereas rails seem to enjoy a dense canopy above their little heads, snipe on the other hand seem to be more at home in shorter cover. This might very well explain why year after year,

On a Snipe Hunt

Any time I mention a snipe hunt, it's always the same look. A mixture of disbelief and concern as if to say, "You're not serious, are you?" Julie's oldest son, Adrian, gave me just such a look when I first asked him if he wanted to go on a snipe hunt near our home in eastern Iowa. "Mom," he told his mother later that evening, "I thought he was going to leave me somewhere. I didn't know you *really* hunted snipe."

To be honest, I don't know whom to blame for this whole snipe-hunting thing. Maybe the Boy Scouts, simply because it always seemed that the Scout leaders were forever taking their young charges out in the dead of night in search of this mythical thing known as the snipe. Or perhaps it's the clan of Old Guys. You know, that same group of old-timers that said things like "Yeah, that old hoop snake'll grab his tail in his mouth and roll like a barrel stave to get away from ya. That's why they call 'em the hoop snake, ya dummy." Or, "Sure 'nough a hummingbird will ride south on the back of a Canada goose. Save 'em the trouble of flyin' now don't it? Ya dummy." Looking back, it sure is amazing the things that these Old Guys know; however, I digress. . . .

So, what exactly is this snipe hunt of legend? The way I understand it, it goes something like this. I, the knowledgeable, invite you, the unknowing, on a snipe hunt. All you'll need, I tell you, is a flashlight or lantern, and a small burlap bag. Then, about midnight, I take you out into the scariest place I can think of, usually a swamp; however, one Old Guy just informed me that his favorite place to take up-and-coming snipe hunters was at the end of an old culvert pipe along some damn near deserted stretch of country road. Regardless of the specifics, the variables are identical—dark and scary. Once I've delivered you, the snipe hunter, to the frightening place, I leave you with these directions: "Hold the light over the bag. Snipe, attracted to the light, will fly into the bag. Once they're in the bag, they can't get out. After a couple hours, I'll come back and get you. Oh, and don't make too much noise or move around 'cause the snipe will see you. And one last thing. Every few minutes, you have to turn the light out. This puts the snipe at ease and makes 'em easier to catch." Then I leave. A couple hours later, I come back, laughing, to find you cowering behind a nearby muskrat house, a jumbled quivering mass of fear. When I catch my breath, I explain that snipe, while real things, aren't caught at night in burlap bags, but are hunted just like pheasants and quail during the light of day. You, apparently in retaliation, hit me—hard—with the beaver stick you've been clutching for the past 60 minutes, and inform me that you plan to continue hating me well past the day of my burial; however, on the walk back to the truck, I hear you ask, "Who can we get next?" And with that, my friend, you've now become a full-fledged snipe hunter.

---

one of the most productive snipe hotspots I've found here in eastern Iowa is a small parcel of corn ground that annually holds a bit of standing water. What's not in standing water is soggy to say the least, and it's here that I'll always find a dozen birds or more on any given outing, particularly if that hunt coincides with the snipe's mid- to late October migration. I'm assuming that it's the ground's lack of tight cover—cover well-suited to the snipe's stubby little green legs—combined with the damp, easily-probed soil that attracts the birds. Too, and similarly so, I've found snipe, often in great numbers, hiding in the ankle-length grass that surrounds many of the periodically flooded low-lying areas around eastern Iowa's wildlife management lands.

The common denominator here? While I wouldn't bypass slightly heavier, more rail-esque covers, where snipe are concerned, I'm thinking short and damp.

Although snipe can commonly be found sharing the same or an adjoining piece of marsh ground with rails, there is one very distinctive characteristic that sets this particular game bird apart from the rails—snipe can fly. I'm not saying that rails are incapable of flight; however, if you hunt them long enough, I can almost guarantee that you'll begin to wonder just how rails accomplish the feat known as migration. Snipe, on the other hand, can put a downwind, just-shot-at mourning dove or blue-wing teal to shame. It all starts with an at-your-feet flush, an act when combined with

Maggie, Jet, and me on a combination rail/snipe hunt in eastern Iowa, otherwise known as playing in the water to escape the heat.

snipe's rather limited vocabulary is the phrase straight line. Once the bird's up, it's all shucking and jiving, bobbing and weaving from there. Yes, eventually this bat-like flight pattern will level out, and usually while the bird's still in more than acceptable shooting range; however, more than one shooter has run himself out of bullets long before this even-keel aspect of the snipe's maneuvers ever takes place. My advice? Wait, if you can, until the bird settles down and flies the way any normal bird should. Or if you can't do that, at least save one shell . . . just in case.

I do want to mention one very interesting note about snipe and flight. For reasons known only to the birds themselves, snipe, on being flushed, will typically fly a large circular path and return to the ground often not more than a few yards from where they originally launched themselves. Often I've watched birds through binoculars, snipe that I was certain were leaving not only the county but also the state, only to have those same birds land but the proverbial stone's throw away from my feet after one or more circles. You want challenging? Try *that* snipe as it passes overhead. In such instances, I've often wished that the shotshell manufacturers would begin making ammunition capable of snipe-like velocities. So far, they're a few hundred feet-per-second behind this incredible little bird.

TAKING UP ARMS

Actually, having read the section on rail guns and gear, I can breeze through this particular segment by simply saying that the same guns and ammunition (non-toxic, remember?) that were put into service for rails can likewise be used for snipe. There's really no difference. Perhaps due to the fact that snipe, as I mentioned, are more than capable aerialists, you might tend to see more 12-gauges in the snipe fields than you will 20s; however, don't let me lead anyone to believe that a 20-gauge filled with steel #7, bismuth #7.5, or Hevi-Shot #9 shot shells—which makes an awesome snipe, dove, woodcock, and quail load, by the way—leaves one, how shall I say, under-gunned when it comes to snipe. No, with snipe, it's not so much in the gun, but in the gunner. Believe me, I've left more than my share of quarter-mile-long trails of Winchester empties in my wake as I chased these silly little birds over a half-section of marshland, but personally, I wouldn't have it any other way.

the snipe's trademark raspy scrape-scrape cry of alarm is often more than enough to unnerve even the steadiest of field veterans. But it doesn't end there, as the snipe's flush is unlike most other game birds. There's no ringneck rise and leveling off. Nor is there anything akin to the timberdoodle's twittering climb through the aspens and alders. Nope. A snipe doesn't so much flush as it's propelled. Top speed, which I'm sure is somewhere between 1,400 and 2,100 feet per second depending upon the ammunition I'm using at the time, is attained immediately upon the bird's feet leaving the ground; still, it gets worse, for nowhere in the

My Pop, Mick (right), and hunting partner, Phil Bourjaily,
with my father's first snipe. He's hooked now.

CHAPTER 11

Snow Removal

IT STARTED AS AN EXPERIMENT AND TURNED into an unforgettable experience. In the spring of 2006, two young men—Tony Vandemore, a Missourian, and Tyson Keller, of Pierre, South Dakota— along with a dedicated cadre of friends set out to answer this both elemental and complex quandary: Is it possible to consistently harvest snow geese over decoys during the Spring Conservation Order, where here the key word is *consistently?* Over the course of 29 days, the group collectively learned not only was it possible, but it was possible 2,030 times.

Scratching your head? Well, let me make you scratch a little harder. Of the more than 2,000 snows the group harvested, the vast majority were mature adults—birds that had experienced not only the Spring Conservation season, but also the traditional fall seasons, some of them for more than 10 years. Long shots? Not hardly. Most of the gunning, I'm told, came at birds cupped and committed, with the average distance being 25 yards. Yes, I said 25 yards.

Now that I've certainly got your full attention, let's take a look at these men, their mission, and just how they found it possible to convince literally thousands of these notoriously "can't kill 'em over decoys" white geese to drop their plastic inhibitions and tumble like so many oak leaves into a huge spread of faux-snows. And remember that word—huge. It's going to be important.

An experiment turned experience, courtesy of two young waterfowlers and tens of thousands of snow geese. PHOTO BY AVERY PRO-STAFF

Above: Missouri's Tony Vandemore with a beautiful banded adult blue goose. *Left:* Tyson Keller, of Pierre, South Dakota, puts the finishing touches on a Greenhead Gear Ground Force blind. BOTH PHOTOS BY AVERY PRO-STAFF

THE MEN

Kirksville, Missouri's Tony Vandemore is an independent insurance agent in his late 20s. His formative years were spent in northwest Illinois, where he claims to have been carried to his father's duck blind while still in diapers. He holds a bachelor's degree in business marketing from Truman State University, and spent time on the San Diego Padres farm team. Vandemore joined the Avery Outdoors Pro-Staff Team in '05, and is the proud "father" of Ruff, a four-year-old black Lab male.

Twenty-five-year-old Tyson Keller also has a bachelor's degree in business marketing, and like his partner, shares a seat with many talented young men and women on the Avery Pro-Staff Team. Keller is three-time South Dakota goose calling champion, and is a former South Dakota state sporting clays champ. A past personal journal entry shows that he hunted Canada geese for "45 straight days," an impressive statistic given the boy was 14 at the time. An enthusiastic outdoor photographer, Keller makes his home in the state capital of Pierre.

THE MISSION

Elementally, the men's mission was to determine if adult snow geese could be deceived—and not simply duped, but fooled completely—using enormous numbers of ultra-realistic full-bodied, hereafter known as FBs, snow and blue goose decoys. Thus armed with 1,600 of Greenhead Gear's (GHG) FB snows, the pair, cronies in tow, set out into the rolling hills of north-central Missouri to make waterfowling history.

What follows are excerpts from conversations I had and very much enjoyed with both of these talented young men.

True or False: There really is no method when you're scouting snows. You simply find a field with birds, and go back the next morning.

Keller: False; there's much more to it. Scouting entails finding the most heavily traveled migration

paths, field preference, feeding area preference, hunting pressure, wind, weather, and observing flock arrangements in the fields. [Note: Keller explains further by definition.]

Migration Paths: Terrain features or bodies of water that serve as a migration highway. Being in line with the birds is crucial.

Field Preference: Pay attention to the stubble height, crop, and topography. This allows for naturalism, and the ability to stay up to date with the birds' feeding habits.

Feeding Area Preference: Sometimes snows will fly miles from the roost to use feeding areas that they are comfortable with. I think it has to do with the abundance of food within a specific area. It's vital that you're in that area.

Hunting Pressure: Birds will often over-fly heavily hunted areas. It's important that you're at the leading edge of the active feeding areas; that is, where the birds are heading, and not where they were.

Changing Wind and Weather: Knowing the birds' habits will allow you to adjust for changing weather. Knowing the migration paths or the feeding routes will allow a hunter to better position himself for the changing conditions.

Flock Arrangement: Birds spread thinly over a field means a minimal food source. Tighter-packed, slow-moving flocks say just the opposite. You want to note the arrangement of the birds within the flocks on the ground; this tells you how to set your own spread.

True or False: There's no reason to hunt afternoons. Afternoons are meant for scouting.

Vandemore: Definitely false. The birds I like to hunt are the migrators, the ones that get up at daylight and leave southeast Missouri. They get up here around two or three o'clock, and they're tired and hungry. Those are the days you wait for. That said, though, we'll always have one or two guys go scout in the afternoon.

Keller: False. Afternoons often provide some of the best migratory activity, with new birds arriving throughout the day. If yours is the only spread when they arrive,

Both men said that scouting played a major role—the major role—in their daily success or lack thereof. PHOTO BY AVERY PRO-STAFF

Mornings weren't always the hot ticket. Often, heavy migration days translated into great afternoon shoots. PHOTO BY AVERY PRO-STAFF

it will show. Sometimes, birds will rest during the morning in periods of heavy migration. In this case, afternoons are the best bet for a solid flight. Typically, though, we do scout during the evenings because finding the evening feed is crucial for the next day's success.

True or False: Size matters when it comes to snows.

Keller: True and False. Snows are often in very large numbers, and (spread) size is critical for high visibility. Too, snows often feel more comfortable dropping into larger numbers of birds.

On the other hand, while we saw that large spreads had great pulling power from long distance, when the birds got close they did not seem to decoy any better to 1,600 over 400. If the birds are already feeding in your area, or there are a large percentage of juvenile birds, smaller numbers will produce well. It really seemed that birds committed better to the spread of 400, and it was much easier to control the birds over 400 decoys.

Vandemore: Realism. It's all about realism.

When you used ALL the decoys, how did you get 1,600 decoys into the field?

Keller: Dry fields meant several pickups and several trailers. Our trucks were each pulling 18 to 24-foot trailers—but we were only able to test the large spreads where and when the fields were dry, and where access was easy and permitted. Otherwise, we relied on four-wheelers to get the spread in and out of the fields.

Where do you begin when you set 1,600 decoys?

Keller: We actually started at the downwind side of the spread. We spaced our decoys further apart at this end, and fingered out many "subgroups" to represent the direction the birds were feeding. As we worked from back to front, we began to pack the decoys tighter to simulate a massive feeding area. The farthest upwind point in the spread was the most tightly packed. We left a hole about 15 to 20 yards in front of our blinds, with the blinds in roughly the front (farthest upwind) 20 yards of the spread.

Is there a system to setting this many decoys?

Keller: We had a couple people driving the trucks in the direction our spread would be set. We would start at the downwind side of the spread and dump piles of 50 to 150 decoys every 30 to 50 yards. Most of the time, Tony and I would design the spread by setting the stakes. Others would follow behind and put the decoys onto the stakes. If too many people were setting the stakes, our spread looked like a jumbled mess.

Tony and I had very similar ideas about decoy placement. Knowing how the spread is assembled helps. Having people follow and put decoys on the stakes is less confusing and much more time efficient.

Is there a configuration you've found particularly effective?

Keller: No specific pattern. We try to keep our set spread out toward the downwind end, with fingers and subgroups. Since snows are very aggressive feeders, we like to keep the decoys extremely tight on the upwind end, usually within inches apart. Our spread with 600 decoys will run about 125 yards long and 30 to 40 yards wide. Roughly 200 decoys will be in the last 20 yards of the spread.

Vandemore: Snows are greedy; they'll go through a field just like a mallard. They're always up and moving,

Talk about realism! PHOTO BY AVERY PRO-STAFF

trying to get ahead of the group. Because of this, nine times out of 10, the geese are going to finish to that tightly packed top end of the spread.

Is there any configuration difference between 400 decoys and 1,600 decoys?

Vandemore: The smaller one is just a "Mini-Me" of the bigger one. Generally, we have a pretty good idea of what we want to accomplish every time we put

How the spread was set depended entirely on what had been seen the night before. This, say the men, is where in-depth scouting comes into play. PHOTO BY AVERY PRO-STAFF

Each of the decoys was set on an Avery RealMotion base, stake or circle base, thus lending motion and movement to the entire spread. PHOTO BY AVERY PRO-STAFF

a decoy stake in the ground. It might seem like there's no method to the madness, that it's just chaos, but we have a good idea of what the final product's going to look like when we start.

Are all of the decoys "movers," or are some stationary?

Keller: All of the decoys were on (GHG) RealMotion bases. Snows are constantly moving, and the motion decoys do a great job duplicating this movement.

Flags?

Keller: Definitely flags. All of our motion is on the upwind side of the spread, where the decoys are most tightly packed. This represents aggressively feeding birds and gave the spread added visibility at distance.

True or False: The guy with 50 FBs and 200 mixed silhouettes and rags can be successful in today's spring snow goose racket.

Keller: They may have a successful day or two, but not consistent success. Smaller makeshift spreads like this may work on an extremely stormy day or on juvenile birds; however, under most circumstances, a spread like that would not get very many looks. Realism is definitely the key. I would be more apt to sit by a waterhole with the 50 FBs than the menagerie.

True or False: White coveralls will work just as well as modern layout blinds for spring snows.

Keller: False. White coveralls often give off ultraviolet radiation, something that the birds have become wise to. To prevent this, our Finisher blinds were constantly mudded to match the surroundings. Any unnatural spot in the field may cause problems.

How important, then, was camouflaging the blinds completely?

Vandemore: The blinds were critical. It's all attention to detail, and we try to improve each time we're out. We like the Finishers because they cover people completely, but then we had to watch—were the doors getting shut all the way? Were things—a blind bag, let's say—left outside that could have used more covering? When you're going to this much effort, there's no sense in half-assing things.

Describe your callers, i.e. the calling units, speakers, cassettes or sound cards.

Keller: Our callers were homemade. We use 400-watt amps for volume; deep cycle batteries for power and longevity. Typically, we'd use two to four Powerhorn speakers per caller box, and MP3s for optimal sound clarity.

How were the callers and speakers positioned within the spread?

Keller: About 70 percent of the speakers were pointed straight up. Since snows usually work straight above the spread, this is where the most sound is needed. If there is wind, we will direct several speakers downwind at a 60-degree angle to hit the on-coming birds. On calm days, we will point a few speakers in various directions, but keep most of them at 60 degrees of incline. Typically, we'll use two callers on the downwind half of the spread, and four in the top one-third.

True or False: There's only one volume necessary for spring snows—loud.

Keller: False. Loud is good, but too loud will actually flare birds. We typically run about 60 percent volume under most conditions. On calmer days, we will turn the callers down. On migration days, higher volumes are favorable. Adjusting the volume to the birds' reactions is the best thing to do. As I mentioned, we

*Even with each individual decoy moving, the men still relied on flags
and flagging to seal the deal.* PHOTO BY AVERY PRO-STAFF

With 1,000 sets of eyes staring at you from 100 yards up, you'd better be hidden. Even Ruff, Vandemore's black Lab, had his own well-camouflaged blind. PHOTO BY AVERY PRO-STAFF

Note the battery box to the left of Tyson Keller. Deep cycle marine batteries, Keller said, were the key to electronic longevity in the field. PHOTO BY AVERY PRO-STAFF

An accomplished trainer, Vandemore says that this spring snow hunt is a fantastic opportunity to work a new or experienced retriever. Ruff, Tony's black Lab, had more than 1,600 retrieves during the 2006 season. PHOTO BY AVERY PRO-STAFF

typically place two or three callers in the last half of the spread on lower volume; higher volume and twice the callers in the front. Snows will fly over the back end and come to the greater number of decoys and higher volume (more noise) at the front end.

True or False: Any cassette or digital device with calling or feeding snow sounds will work just fine.

Keller: False. Clarity is the most important aspect; that's why we use the MP3s. Too, you want to find sounds with more individual birds instead of the loud, massive roar. Mixing several callers with several individual bird sounds has proven to be the most successful. An equal mix of calling and feeding sounds is preferable.

Do you accompany the electronics with mouth calling?

Keller: We only use mouth calls during the fall season. In the spring, it's entirely e-callers.

You used dogs this spring. How did you hide them? And how did you work with them?

Vandemore: We used Finisher dog blinds all spring. A lot of guys will put their dogs behind them. I like to

have mine—the dog blind—slightly behind and touching my blind. Ruff's pretty steady, but some dogs aren't. The way I have mine positioned, I can talk to him ("easy" . . . "steady") if I need to, plus he's tracking birds right down the gun barrel. It's a safety thing, too. When you have three honkers come in, you shoot three times and everything's dead. But with 1,000 snows and a dog that breaks, the first shot goes off and he's 20 yards into the decoys where everything's happening. It's not good. Plus, spring snow goose hunting is an incredible opportunity to get dog work in. Heck, this season, Ruff picked up right at 1,600 geese.

What makes you guys different and consistently successful on spring snows?

Vandemore: Scouting, and not half-assing anything. And we had to commit to long hours. [Note: The boys averaged roughly three hours of sleep a night for 30 straight days. And meals? All were on the run.]

Keller: Hard work. Most days we would get up at 4:45 A.M., hunt until late morning, and scout on the way back to eat lunch. We'd go back to the spread, hunt the afternoon, send a couple trucks scouting, and re-set

Scenes such as this were possible only through attention to detail, including blinds and concealment. PHOTO BY AVERY PRO-STAFF

That's Vandemore (front), and Keller (second from right). Just look at 'em. If I were a white goose, I'd stay in the Arctic year-round. PHOTO BY AVERY PRO-STAFF

Where will snow goose hunting be in the Year 2020? No one, not even these talented young men, knows for certain. PHOTO BY AVERY PRO-STAFF

the spread after dark. Constantly repositioning the spread was major because we were always where the birds were. Keeping an eye on the flight patterns, how the geese positioned in the fields, and feeding/migrating areas accounted for the majority. A lifelike spread accompanied by realistic sounds also was key.

When the birds wise up to FBs, what's next?

Keller: I can't answer that question. I guess constant innovation will lead us into the future of hunting. I can say that the FBs have definitely revolutionized decoying snow geese.

Vandemore: It's hard to fathom what's going to be next, but there's always going to be innovation. I'm sure [he laughs] that people are looking at building

a better mousetrap; that being said, a goose is still a goose. He's got to eat to stay alive, and he's going to migrate. And anytime you have geese needing to feed, you're always going to be able to kill some.

What does one do with 2,030 snow geese once they're in the back of the truck?

Vandemore: We had people in place—needy families, church pantries, soup kitchens—to take the birds before we started hunting. Snow goose is by no means poor table fare; it's actually very good. With snows, you can pick out the (gray) juvenile birds a lot easier and concentrate on those. But I had folks lined up who would take just about every snow goose we could take to 'em.

CHAPTER 12

Back to (Shooting) School

A LTHOUGH I'M SURE THERE EXISTED
shooting schools during the time I was growing up in northeast Ohio in the mid-1970s,
I'd never heard of them. No, I take that back; I had
heard of them. They were called the Mick Johnson
School of Shotgun Shooting. And the Jim Johnson
School. And the Neal Verity School. And the Dzedo
Johnson Shooting School. Those men, by the way,
were Dad, Uncle, Uncle, and Grandpa.

Back then, school was a place a kid went Monday
through Friday until he turned 18. Then he either
went to work in one of the steel mills in the Mahon-
ing Valley, or he went to college where he wore scarlet
and gray and cheered for The Buckeyes in The Horse-
shoe on Saturday afternoons in the fall. Shotgun
shooting was something that he learned at home; or
rather, in the field, and not at the hands of a smartly
dressed Brit or penny loafer-wearing psychologist who
just so happened to be armed with a vintage O/U.
Nope, shooting skills were taught, to use the term
loosely, by Dad or by Grandpa. Maybe an uncle or the
neighbor down the way, if a relative wasn't available.
Unless I'm mistaken, instruction back in the day con-
sisted primarily of very simple rules. One, don't shoot
your teacher. Two, keep both eyes open. And three,

With instruction, a poor shooter can become a good shooter—and a good shooter, even better.

shoot where the bird's going, not where it's been. End of story . . . school's out.

Gun fit back then was simple, too. You put the butt plate or recoil pad in the crook of your elbow, and if your finger reached the trigger . . . well, then the gun fit. Back then, there were only two kinds of shooters. Those who hit what they shot at, also known as good shots, and those who couldn't hit the proverbial broad side of a barn. From the inside, nonetheless. These were the men that the good shots talked about, and that's just the way it was.

Today, though, the scene is quite different. Shooting instruction—shooting schools or clinics, if you will—are quite popular, not to mention quite effective in helping men, women, and children alike become more efficient shotgunners. And before you ask, the answer is a definite no; these courses and clinics aren't attended only by professional or competitive trap, skeet, and sporting clays shooters, but often by the average, every-day hunter in the field—someone who simply wants to leave the ranks of the bad shots and join the ranks, even if only occasionally, of the good shots.

A native Texan, Gil Ash, and his wife and teaching partner, Vicki, are what most would call the good shots. Gil, 55, was born in Madisonville, Texas, though he lived most of his life in the Dallas area. He attended East Texas State University where he earned a degree in photography and business. Upon his graduation, Ash borrowed $300, rented a U-Haul trailer, and as he says "went to Houston to seek his fortune." He started his own commercial photography business, and the rest, as he says, is history; that is, until his path crossed that of a young lady by the name of Vicki.

Many waterfowlers could benefit from a formal shooting lesson; myself very much included. PHOTO BY AVERY PRO-STAFF

"I didn't grow up in a very well-to-do family, and my father's boss bought me a Remington Model 1100 16-gauge when I was 14 or 15 years old," remembers Ash. "I shot that gun for years. I took up the game of skeet, and at that time, you couldn't get any reloading components for the 16-gauge. I loved to shoot skeet, so I sold the 16-gauge. I traded it in on a 20-gauge so I could reload for it. This was just about the time Vicki and I started to date.

"Well," he continued, "she started shooting with me, and her Daddy bought her a shotgun and had it cut. And we started hunting together, and we went on a dove hunt. We were sitting by a little pond and I'd missed a few birds, and I said, 'You know, if I had that little 16-gauge, I would have killed that bird.' This is in September and we'd been dating about 30 days. She went down to the gun shop that I traded that gun into and she bought that gun back. She kept it and gave it to me for Christmas. The following August we were married. You might say we had a shotgun wedding. Not the normal shotgun wedding."

That so-called shotgun wedding was in 1975. In the years following the nuptials, the Ashes spent much of time afield, both on the range and hunting a variety of upland birds in their native Texas. It was during this time, too, that the couple found a new addiction— sporting clays. From 1983 through 1987, the Ashes toured much of the United States shooting sporting clays on a competitive level.

"Because we were from out of town and because we won the tournaments," said Ash, "people wanted to know how we did it. We quickly got the reputation for being able to teach people to do it. By the late 1980s and early 1990s, we began to teach more than we would compete. In 1993, I tore a rotator cuff in my shoulder and couldn't shoot. So I began to study how to teach because I wanted to stay involved. In 1992, Vicki won the ladies' division of the national sporting clays championship. We began to teach more, and our teaching schedule began to grow rapidly. Vicki and I are both Level 3 certified NSCA (National Sporting Clays Association) instructors. I was in the first NSCA Level 3 course that was given, and I was one of two out of 12 people who passed it. Vicki was in the third or fourth course."

Perhaps not surprisingly, this love for both the shotgunning sports and teaching eventually lead to the

Professional shooting instructor Gil Ash, together with his wife, Vicki, own and operate Optimum Shooting Performance (OSP). PHOTO BY PHIL BOURJAILY

Ashes creating their own shooting school—Optimum Shooting Performance (OSP) of Houston, Texas.

"We teach about 2,000 people a year," said Ash. "Since beginning our business in 1995, we've seen in excess of 4.5 million shotgun shells fired at clay targets and game birds. When you see that much, certain patterns begin to emerge. Certain patterns that create success with a shotgun, and certain patterns that create risk with a shotgun. We began to realize that there is a lot more to shooting a shotgun than just telling people where they missed."

With this educational experience in mind, it seemed fitting that we sit with Ash for a spell and talk with him about the whats and whys of the modern shotgun shooting school, not forgetting that one most important question: Is shooting school for me?

MDJ: Who are your students?

Ash: Of the 2,000 people that we teach each year, 60 percent of them will never shoot a tournament or a registered target. They enjoy shooting. They're recreational shooters. And they're hunters. They love to shoot shotguns at clay targets and make noise and break things.

The person we see often is the person who used to shoot a lot when they were growing up. And they were a really good shot. Now they're 45 to 60. They have some disposable income, they remember how fun hunting used to be, and they want to start hunting again. And they can't hit anything. They go on a corporate dove hunt or they go hunting with their buddies, and they're embarrassed because it takes 'em a box of shells to kill one bird. They come to us saying "There's something wrong with my eyes. I've lost my timing. I just can't hit anything anymore."

When they were a kid, they just looked at a bird and they shot it. Now that they're a success and they've trained their conscious doubt voice to doubt everything they do, they try to look at the gun and they try to check the lead. They're trying to make sure the lead is right before they pull the trigger, and when you do that, you're going to miss.

MDJ: How about a "for instance"?

Ash: You're sitting under a tree on a stool picking your nose in a dove field, and someone yells "Over ya!" You look up, mount the gun, shoot, and stone the bird. Then you see one a'coming 200 yards away. You stand up: Gun on shoulder? Check. Cheek on stock? Check. Beads lined up? Check. Boom-boom-boom-damn! That's the difference between conscious and subconscious function. Your focus was on the barrel and not on the bird, and that's why you miss. That's why most people kill their birds on the second shot.

MDJ: What about men versus women? Do you see one more often than the other?

Ash: We teach from 10 to 15 percent women. The people that actually come to take a shooting lesson come to learn, male and female. The problem with women is many don't have the upper body strength to hold a shotgun up. Women have to work at two things in opposite order. First, they have to work on their upper body strength so they can hold a shotgun up long enough to learn. Second and most importantly, women have to develop a timing database.

Most women have no timing database. When you were a kid, you played those games that typically have to do with timing; many women don't have that. Give me someone who was an athlete in high school or college, and they have a timing database. Our task is to get women to understand the rhythm and timing of shotgun shooting. Get them to develop a good gun mount, and the timing database that's already in their brain can be converted over to shooting a shotgun. A woman has to learn to develop that database *and* shoot a shotgun at the same time.

MDJ: How does the clinic actually begin?

Ash: After we watch a student shoot one bird, we'll tell them what their normal score is. What birds they can hit, and what birds they can't hit. This after shooting one shot. And sometimes we can tell these things before they yell "pull." Then we'll take the group over to a target that we know they can't hit, and we'll have everybody in the group shoot five. They'll break five in a row. Then we'll take the person in the group that the group sees as being the least experienced, and we'll have them break five in a row. Then we'll take the person who's reluctant to change—who's missing—and we'll keep feeding them bullets. Sooner or later, they're going to turn around and ask, "Why can't I hit this target?" We call that the teachable moment.

MDJ: Gil, talk about instinctive shooting.

Ash: Webster defines instinctive as happening below consciousness. We teach instinctive shooting. Most people look at instinctive shooting on the clays course as you get in the cage, you call pull, you mount the gun, and you shoot at the birds. That's instinctive, but there's no rhyme or reason for that type of shooting. What we teach is this: You have to move and mount the shotgun precisely. Once you master those mechanics and you master a couple of moves, then regardless of what the bird does in the field, all you have to do in the field is mount the gun, look at the bird, and pull the trigger.

MDJ: Can attending a shooting school actually worsen a person's shooting?

Ash: Everything new feels strange until it becomes old. For you to correct your problem, we have to first show you the problem and why it creates risk. Then we have to show you how to practice to eliminate that chink in your armor. Then you must practice it. And once you've practiced it, then you'll become a better shooter.

Class schedules shouldn't be grueling; still, there's quite a bit to be accomplished in a short period of time. Get a good night's sleep, and be on your toes come sunrise. PHOTO BY PHIL BOURJAILY

Your question to me was, Can taking your course screw me up as a shooter? Definitely, because the only way you're going to get better is to change what you're doing. Nobody likes to change because they're afraid of the failure that can come with change. The last thing you should expect when you go take a shooting lesson is for you to end up a great shot, because you have to learn what's wrong and how to correct it. Then you have to correct it, and after you've practiced it, then you become a better shooter.

MDJ: Everything I see about shooting schools shouts formal. Are formal and shooting school synonymous terms?

Ash: If you're looking for formal, go somewhere else. I wear sandals, running shorts, and a Polo shirt. You have to dress with the climate. We're outdoors from 8 in the morning 'til 5 in the afternoon, and if we try to be too formal, you're getting so hot that you can't see by 2 o'clock in the afternoon.

MDJ: Will shooting school help me as a hunter?

Ash: Most dramatically. The way it helps you in the field . . . one, when you're having a bad day or you miss a shot, you'll know why. But more importantly, people that take instruction shoot more often. They spend more time on the clays range or the skeet range or the trap range, and they practice their moves and they work on their proficiency as a shooter. Therefore when they go to the field, they're more proficient. And if they're more proficient in moving and mounting their gun, they'll spend more time on target focus in part because, after a course, they know the importance of target focus. They instantly become better wingshooters.

When we have field hunters come in and they start missing, here's what we tell 'em. We tell 'em to watch three to five birds fly by and don't shoot at them. Focus on them. Focus on the heads. Point at 'em with your finger. Realize how slow they're moving. Then when they start shooting at them again, they'll only load one bullet until they break one bird. Then they'll load two. That third shot, you might as well throw it away.

Shooting proficiency is the cornerstone for the ethical harvest of all wildlife. Sooner or later, we as hunters are going to have to look at our proficiency in the field and look at it for what it is. We're going to have to look at what we're doing—how we're shooting—or we're going to have a problem with the anti-hunters.

MDJ: Is shooting more often an effective way to improve, or is it simply shooting more often?

Ash: We've done some studies on shooting more often, and we found that the students that we have that do two things—practice what we tell them or teach them to practice, and go to the range at least two times a week for the three weeks following the clinic—they'll retain over 80 percent of what we taught them. The people who don't do these things retain from 25 to 40 percent. These people will retain what we teach them intellectually, but they can't apply it. You can't be thinking about swing mechanics when the bird's in the air. The swing mechanics have to be in the subconscious.

The physical therapists and neurologists tell us that you have to have done something 2,500 to 3,000 times, and done it correctly, before it's embedded in the subconscious. And instinctive shooting is nothing more than subconscious shooting. Now you can be subconscious without good mechanics, and not be a very good shot. But if you have good subconscious mechanics, you're going to be lethal.

MDJ: When would you recommend attending a shooting school?

Ash: We recommend that you take a shooting lesson a minimum of 30 days before you're going to go hunting. People come to us three days before they go quail hunting, and they expect us to make 'em a great quail shot. It's not going to happen. We can talk to them about fundamentals and we can help them with their gun mount, but once they go out after we've talked to them and they shoot better and more proficiently, then they want to start four weeks or six weeks out . . . before next season.

MDJ: I'm new to the shooting sports and I don't as yet have a shotgun. Should I purchase before going to a school, or will there be shotguns there that I can use and evaluate?

Ash: We have guns for people to use, but we would recommend prior to coming to an all-day clinic, you

All students, regardless of skill level, need to remember one thing: Shooting is supposed to be fun.

come spend a couple hours with us. We'll work on your gun mount; we'll get you into a gun.

As for a gun, it all depends on how much money you want to spend and what kind of commitment you want to make. If you want to spend $500 on a gun 'cause you want to go dove hunting a couple times a year and, with the clinic, you want to be a little more proficient, then maybe a pump-gun or a semi-automatic. Something that's functional in the field. On the other hand, if you want a nice O/U, nice O/Us go from $1,400 to $140,000. It depends on what you want to spend. We can arrange for you to try different guns before you buy them, but the most important thing we're going to do as teachers is not tell you what you're going to buy, but we're going to educate you in the different types of shotguns that are available—and then you can make your own decision.

MDJ: How critical is gun fit to successful shotgun shooting, and what role does that play in a shooting school?

Ash: We do from 150 to 200 gun fits a year. Gun fit is important, to a certain extent. If a gun is too long for an individual or too short for an individual, that's very important. But the quality of the gun fit is tied directly to the ability of the person shooting the gun to move it and mount it consistently. We do two gun fits. We do a complete and thorough gun fit for a person who has a good move and a good mount. Then we have what we call a novice gun fit for someone who cannot move and mount the gun. The novice gun fit is to adjust the pull and pitch, and put a little drop and a little cast in the stock, so that the person can shoot the gun without it hurting them. It's then the person's job to go and shoot the gun a couple thousand rounds, then they'll come back, we'll go to the pattern plate, and we'll finish up the gun fit.

It's like this. If you were to come to me and want me to build you a custom set of golf clubs, but you'd only played golf three times in your life, you don't have the ability to swing the clubs consistently enough to appreciate the nuances that a custom set of clubs provides. You don't swing the clubs consistently enough for me to adjust the shaft length to $1/16$ of an inch. It's the same thing with shotguns. There are some people out there who will tell you that gun fit is the number one priority. It's not. A lot of gun fit problems can be cured with a good gun mount, and I think that any

When you take shooting instruction, says Ash, can have an influence on how you improve—or slip backwards—when in the field. PHOTO BY PHIL BOURJAILY

gun-fitter worth his salt would agree with that statement. Vicki and I routinely demonstrate shots with students' guns. We demonstrate them right-handed and we demonstrate them left-handed. The length of pulls on those guns can range from 12.5 inches to 17 inches, but because we have a good gun mount, we can consistently mount the gun well and break those targets so the students can see how to do that.

MDJ: What is the most difficult shooting concept, for lack of a better phrase, for your students to grasp?

Ash: Moving the muzzle with the target. Let's say you're shooting at left to right target at 20 yards, and the target takes three of lead. If you move and mount the gun with that bird and the gun's three feet ahead of the bird, but the gun's going twice as fast as the bird—when you pull the trigger, what's going to happen? You're going to shoot ahead of the bird. Now, same scenario,

Proper gun fit? Proper mount? A trained shooter instructor can help determine the answers to these and other shooting-related questions.

but now the gun's going half as fast as the target. What then? You're going to shoot behind the target.

It's not the lead that's important. It's whether or not the muzzle speed is equal to the bird's speed because then and only then is the right lead the right lead. We call that tempo. Tempo is the most common misconception in shotgunning. People want to get the gun up, run and chase, find the bird, triangulate the lead, and shoot. What ends up happening is the birds appear to fly three times faster than they're really flying.

Watch someone shoot sporting clays. When you're watching, the birds seem to fly slow. Then when you're in the cage, the birds seem to speed up. The engineers call this relative velocity—how fast something appears to fly. We call it visual speed. We're standing on the edge of the highway watching the cars go by at 70 miles per hour. They seem to be going awful fast. Now, we get in your pickup truck and we start going 70 miles per hour. The traffic seems to slow down.

MDJ: Is there a bottom line to shotgunning and shooting schools?

Ash: Shooting is just like putting a new program in your computer. You have to learn about it before you can use it, and before you can do it instinctively. It doesn't matter if it's fly-casting, learning to walk . . . it just doesn't matter; you have to do it. We sum it up this way. Technical expertise is always preceded by experience. In order to do something well, we must have done it many times.

MDJ: What should I expect during a day-long shotgunning clinic with you folks?

Ash: You're going to shoot somewhere between seven and ten boxes of shells, depending upon the types of targets we're shooting that day. We'll start in the morning and we'll talk to the group. Vicki will divide the people into two groups, and she'll let me know what my group has to work on. She'll take a group, and we'll each start with one fundamental crossing target, probably a simple left-to-right or right-to-left target. You'll walk up to the target and shoot five or six times doing what you normally do. Don't try to impress me; just do what you normally do. I'll make notes on your card, not as to what your perception of the problem is, but what your *real* problem is.

MDJ: Large groups? Small groups?

Ash: Number? Vicki will take five people, and I'll take five. Five's the magic number. If you take six, they don't get to shoot enough. If you take four, they end up going brain-dead about 3:15. If you take five, they go brain-dead about 4:16, plus or minus a minute. And they're not physically tired. They're mentally tired. In a group scenario, you learn more from watching others shoot than you do actually pulling the trigger.

If everyone has a common problem, which they normally do, we'll start to work with the first shooter. Get them to slow down. Look at the bird before they move. Move and mount with the speed of the bird, and hit the bird. Then the next shooter has watched the first, and they're ready. Finally the last shooter, it usually only takes them two or three shots before they're there. Then we go to another target. Eventually, we train these shooters to instinctively react to what the target does.

MDJ: And as the day continues?

Ash: About 10:45 to 11:00, it clicks. People begin to understand why they miss when they miss, and why they hit when they hit. Each person will have a unique problem that we will deal with throughout the day. By lunchtime, the people are slapping high-fives. They're amazed at how slow the birds are, and they're amazed at how easy the birds are to hit. They're amazed at how much they've been looking at the gun, and how looking at the gun prevents them from being successful.

After lunch, we may pattern the guns on the pattern plates, or we'll talk about gun fit. Then we'll go back to shooting; maybe some slow targets to give them time to move and mount the gun and be successful. Mid-afternoon, and depending on what the group needs, we might shoot pairs. We might shoot report pairs. We might shoot doubles. If the group's coming along well or they're experienced shooters, we might move back and shoot 40-, 50-, or 60-yard crossers. We'll get them to believe that they can hit those birds without checking the lead.

MDJ: A typical price and timeframe for this instruction?

Ash: In 2005, the price is $350 a day, plus your targets and your ammo. You can bring your own ammo or you can purchase that at the club. Targets are 30 cents apiece, and you'll end up shooting roughly 200 targets. We typically recommend that people, if they can, come for two days. The first day is typically deprogramming; the second day is typically reprogramming. If we know you can only be there for one day, about 2 o'clock in the afternoon we will shift what we're doing for you so as to begin the imprinting phase of our teaching. We'll begin to say things in a different way to you, and we'll begin to point out specific things you need to practice and why you need to practice them.

If this is you, then about 2 o'clock, I'd begin to take you to targets that were your weak points. I would coach you on these targets, and I would emphasize how important it is for you to become a better shooter, for you to conquer the two or three things that I'm pointing out to you. I would tell you how to practice and how often to practice. I'll tell you that if you will do what I'm telling you to do—shoot at least two times a week for the next three weeks, doing this the first week and this the second week and this the third week—this problem we're discussing will go away.

Here, let's shift our focus away from the teacher and speak for a moment to one of OSP's former students, Philip Bourjaily. Currently living in Iowa City, Iowa, Bourjaily, 46, serves as the shooting editor for *Field & Stream,* and as such, along with his passion for English pointers and upland wingshooting, spends more than his fair share of time behind the butt plate of a shotgun. And with that . . .

MDJ: Why would an experienced shooter such as you attend a shooting school?

Bourjaily: Why would a major league ball player go to the batting cages or to his batting coach? I'm not saying that I'm at that level of shooting—I'm not—but everybody, regardless of his or her level of ability, can improve. Everybody goes into slumps. Everybody needs work on the mental end of his or her game. There's a lot that shooting coaches can do for you.

MDJ: And as a hunter? Has formal shooting instruction proved effective?

Bourjaily: I've learned a lot. We practiced some long-range shooting at the last OSP clinic I attended. They told me that the secret to long-range shooting is to move the gun very slowly, which seems wrong. But I was able to put that into practice in Canada, and shot geese at ranges that I'd just as soon not reveal.

MDJ: How was your personal style of shooting affected by this professional instruction, or was it?

Bourjaily: The two things that the Ashes picked on me for . . . one was riding targets. That is, staying with the targets too long to make sure my lead was right. The longer you stay with the target, the greater the chance you're going to slow the gun and miss. Like every shooting instructor I've ever worked with has emphasized, when the gun comes to your cheek and shoulder, that's

It's taken me years to learn to shoot this Model 24 16-gauge well; however, with time and advice from several skilled shooters, I'm much more efficient with this particular piece.

when you pull the trigger. When you check and double-check your lead like I was doing, the only thing that lies down that path is misses and frustration.

The other thing, which I was initially surprised about but which made sense once they explained it to me, was that I follow through too much. I have a very conscious push of the gun following the shot, which I'm sure is a habit left over from bird hunting. The Ashes said that what happens here is that the shooter begins relying too much on that exaggerated follow through in order to get the gun out in front of the target rather than putting the muzzle in the right place the first time. Sooner or later, you will begin to miss if you begin to rely on that conscious follow through.

One of the things that I got out of shooting with the Ashes, and watching them shoot, is that very good shooters are very economical with their movement. That really impressed me quite a bit.

MDJ: Has shooting instruction helped you to improve in the field?

Here, Ash explains some of the finer points of shotgunning to Field & Stream *shooting editor, Phil Bourjaily.* PHOTO BY PHIL BOURJAILY

Bourjaily: Perhaps the most significant thing you take away from any shooting lesson is that you learn to diagnose your own misses. You learn to answer the question, Why did I miss? And that's very important to become a better shooter, whether that's on the range or in the field. Yes, clay targets don't have wings that flap and they slow down versus speeding up; still, hitting a moving target is hitting a moving target. There is a lot of carry-over from a clinic to the field.

MDJ: And practice after instruction?

Bourjaily: You can go to a clinic and you can shoot really well with someone standing at your elbow handing you bullets and telling you what to do, but if you don't follow through and practice, it's all for naught. And you need to practice a specific way or you'll lose a lot of what they'll teach you. And practicing the right way isn't going to the gun club and shooting a couple rounds of skeet. You go to the gun club when there's nobody there, and you shoot a couple boxes of shells at whatever target or targets that give you trouble.

MDJ: Is there any type of mental preparation a shooter might want to consider prior to enrolling in a shooting school?

Bourjaily: You need to be ready to admit that you might be doing it wrong. Anybody who has shot as long as you or I have [Note: That would be approximately a combined 53 years] has developed bad habits. Instructors would much rather work with someone who has never picked up a shotgun before. It's amazing what they can do with a total beginner. With us, they have to break down the bad habits. What most instructors have told me is that they like to have somebody for two days. The first day is spent breaking the bad habits, and the second day is spent instilling the new ones.

MDJ: And as a student, your bottom line on shooting schools?

Bourjaily: These shooting clinics are fun. Taking lessons is just fun, as long as you don't let your ego get in the way. Gil uses a lot of humor and a lot of sarcasm—in a good-natured way—in his clinics, and he keeps it fun. You find yourself doing things that you really didn't think you could do, and that's neat too. You have to go into these clinics with an open mind and be ready to admit that some of the things you thought were right aren't necessarily right. If you do that, you'll get a lot of benefit out of the lesson.

*Does formal training have merit for the shotgunner looking to become
more skilled afield? According to Gil Ash, most definitely.*

CHAPTER 13

The Goose Gurus

TWO THOUSAND WORDS MAY SOUND LIKE a mountain of letters for those of you who don't write for a living. Hell, it's a pile for those of us who do—that is, most of the time. Some subjects just don't lend themselves to brevity. Tolstoy's editor didn't tell him, "Hey, Leo. Let's keep this *War & Peace* thing to under, say, 5,000 words, eh?" And it'd be safe to say that Melville didn't have a word count hanging over his head while we worked on *Moby Dick,* now did he?

But I faced a similar challenge with this topic— The Goose Gurus. Within each of the men featured here dwell hundreds of thousands of words, every one of them focusing on the art that is modern goose hunting. Assembled are champions, innovators, callers, and comedians; they're decoy carvers, blind builders, farmers, family men, and former commercial clammers. Their strategies—which make them the best in the business—are difficult, if not impossible, to distill into mere paragraphs, yet that's what we've done. Here, then, is The Reader's Digest Condensed Version of The Goose Gurus—the very best from the very best. Class is now in session.

FRED ZINK
An Ohio boy like me, Zink knows more about the biological makeup of the Canada goose—that is, why geese do what they do—than anyone at present; that's why the

Is that what the Goose Gurus pursue with such conviction, the Bird with the Golden Band? PHOTO BY AVERY PRO-STAFF

Ohioan Freddie Zink, one of the best in the business and in the field, and owner of Zink Calls.

guy's good at what he does, and that's decoy honkers. Zink's the owner of Zink Calls (www.zinkcalls.com), and works full-time in product design and development for Avery Outdoors (www.averyoutdoors.com). His calling prowess is legendary.

Zink on freelancing: If you're a freelance goose hunter on the run, don't get caught up on all the gadgetry; work on the basics when hunting educated geese. Don't overlook the importance of hiding well. You have to put some effort into it. Select the lowest possible ground blind you can fit in. Mud it according to the manufacturer's suggestions. And stubble the blind correctly. Don't get lazy here; *always* use stubble or grass from the field you're going to be hunting, not just the stubble that's on

there from the day before. Finally, use the terrain features of the field you're going to hunt to help hide you and the blinds.

CHAD BELDING
Belding is Larry the Cable Guy, only smarter and funnier—and, if you ask him, he'll tell you much better looking; he's also a better waterfowl caller. With current digs in Sparks, Nevada, he's a two-time winner of the state duck calling championships, and has walked away with the state goose calling trophy on three different occasions. In addition to working with Avery Outdoors and Zink Calls, he owns or is partial owner of three separate business ventures in the West, making him the James Brown of the hunting industry.

Belding on in-depth scouting: Everyone talks scouting, but not everyone does it right. You need to answer all the questions. Where are the roosts? This will help if, for whatever reason, you can't be on the X—you can put yourself between the roost and the field the geese are using. What will the wind be doing after sun-up? A lot of times, there's no wind before daylight, but it will come up later in the morning. You watch the Weather Channel or get on the Internet and find out that wind direction so you can set up right even with no wind. What's the weather 300 miles or so to the north? This can help you decide on the number of decoys, or even if you need to bring additional callers so those high migrating birds can hear you.

SHAWN STAHL

Hailing from Allegan, Michigan, Shawn Stahl possesses the patience of a saint, a personality trait he demonstrated when he worked with me—and didn't threaten my life—to define more than 50 goose calling terms a couple years back for a project I was given. Today, the 2000 World Goose Calling Champ runs his Gander Hill Productions, filming his Fowl Pursuit Series (www.fowlpursuit.com) of waterfowl videos.

Stahl on the fundamentals: When you're learning to use a short reed call, it's important to master *all* of the fundamental mechanics of operating a short reed.

Michigan's Shawn Stahl—calling champ and owner of Gander Hills Productions.

Building a strong foundation will allow you to do all the advanced work later. Too often, callers want to rush right into something like double clucking before they're mastered proper air control and hand position—and these are the two most critical aspects to doing the double cluck correctly.

There are two types of callers: people-pleasers, and goose-getters. What's appealing to the human ear isn't always what Mother Nature likes to hear. Some of the best field callers I know couldn't call a judge to a buffet, but they take top honors in the field more days than not.

SCOTT THREINEN

Threinen, like Stahl, has the patience of Job—I made the boy famous in a book, but spelled his name wrong. "Easy come, easy go," he told me. Threinen's calling resume includes the 2002 Minnesota State goose calling championship, the 2002 Galyans Open, and the

Chad Belding of Sparks, Nevada—competitive goose caller, self-made millionaire, and funnyman extraordinaire.

Above: Nugent ain't got nothin' on the Minnesota Maniac, Scott "Did you spell my name right?" Threinen. Excellent caller, and all-round great kid. PHOTO BY SCOTT THREINEN
Right: The Godfather of Goose, Tim Grounds. As good as they come, and the man responsible for many of the calls and calling styles we're using now. PHOTO BY JUDA GROUNDS

2005 World Team Goose with partner Kelley Powers. He's a fantastic young man, and a hell of a goose hunter. You'll be seeing more of him in the future.

Threinen on calling and hunting pressure: Today, we deal with hunting pressure in a number of ways—changing our location, the number of decoys we set, or the way we call. But no matter what we change, we still have the same human tendencies, especially in our calling. We may change how much we call, but we're still playing the same notes over and over again; we do this in the field, and geese hear this. So when the pressure's on, instead of changing *how much* you call, switch up the notes, the calling sequences, and most of all, *when* you actually start to call to the birds.

TIM GROUNDS

I once described Tim Grounds (www.timgrounds.com) as "The Godfather of Goose," and I'm going to stick to that description here. Grounds's are the footsteps in which many of today's goose hunting notables first walked, and in which many still stride. Today he's enjoying life in southern Illinois, spending time on the tournament bass fishing circuit with his son, Hunter, who's not too shabby a goose caller himself.

Grounds on versatility: The most important thing, especially with calling but with everything associated with goose hunting, is to be versatile. There are lots of guys out there who can blow a goose call, but they don't know geese. I've been in this business 31 years now, and I learn something new every year. You're never too old to learn, and you're never too good to learn. You've got to keep an open mind.

As for calling, you don't want to throw all your cards on the table at once. There's a time for going ballistic with the call, like some guys do. It's the Wall of Sound, as I call it. Basically, though, call low-high and high-low, just like that goose and gander calling back and forth. If you can cluck and moan *and* you know geese, you can kill birds.

RON LATSCHAW

One has only to say the word "Eliminator" among a gathering of goose chasers, and the topic turns immediately to Oregon resident Ron Latschaw. In 1993, Latschaw rocked the waterfowling world with his introduction of the first portable, lightweight low-profile ground blind, and it's been a wild ride for him and his company, Final Approach, ever since.

Latschaw on late-season decoy spreads: Late season, my spreads change by numbers. I'll often put out just eight decoys; that's kind of my magic number. When geese commit and come into an eight-decoy spread, they're right there. I mean everybody's going to have a shot at 'em. You're not all spread across the rig. You put out 100 decoys, and those birds can land on the left side. They can land on the right side. It's magic when they come into eight decoys. They've had it. There's no getting away from you.

I'll put out three feeders, four sentinels, and maybe one resting bird. That's it. One resting bird, three heads down and four heads up. And it's interesting that the birds that are cautious and are in the bigger groups find these small decoy spreads really interesting. They come right down to 'em.

FIELD HUDNALL

I'm sincere when I say you'd be hard-pressed to meet a nicer young man than Field Hudnall. A Kentuckian by birth, Field, and his brother Clay, both work with Freddie Zink at the now Port Clinton, Ohio-based call company. In length, Hudnall's competitive history reads like Tolstoy's *War & Peace*: 2005 Winchester World Open Goose; 2005 International Invitational Goose; 2004 World Goose; 2004 North American Two-man Goose; 2004 Bass Pro/Redhead Open Goose; 2003 and 2005 Ohio State Goose Calling Champion; 2003 Canadian-American International Two-Man Goose; and on.

Hudnall on intensity: Many hunters feel intimidated by the hype that comes with the short reed goose call. When they start hearing things like push moans, double spit notes, and quiver moans, it can intimidate the most experienced caller. While sounds like these do exist in contest calling, let's face it—most of us just want to call in a goose to shoot. And to be honest, that double quiver push moan on the rocks with a twist isn't going to call a goose any better than good, old sharp aggressive clucks.

If you want to get better, practice calling at different levels of intensity—not different sounds. Learn how to go from deep relaxed sounds to high aggressive sounds in a split-second. Changing the intensity of your calling while performing the same notes is by far more effective than changing the notes but not the intensity.

Mister Eliminator, Oregon's Ron Latschaw, in a duck hunting moment. PHOTO BY FA BRANDS

BILL SAUNDERS

Saunders (www.guideseriescalls.com) has done for the Pacific Northwest what Grounds did in the Midwest; he started a goose calling revolution that hasn't slowed down in the past decade. I find Bill quiet—other folks don't; what we all agree on is the man's ability with a goose call, talents that include three-time Washington State goose calling champion, four-time Pacific Flyway Regional Champion, and more than 25 first-place finishes. He's a good walleye fisherman, too.

Saunders on calling the subspecies: I like to say "match the hatch" when hunting different subspecies of Canada geese; that is, match your calling to the geese at hand. When hunting honkers, I use my Reload or original Guide Series for a deeper, more mellow tone. I also make my tempo slow and deliberate. I'll change to my Traffic call when lessers are the target. It's a higher pitched call, and I pick up my tempo, too. High/low clucking and scratchy clucks

Evergreen Stater Bill Saunders, there in the middle surrounded by Pacific Wings owner Mike Franklin (left) and Final Approach founder Ron Latschaw. PHOTO BY BILL SAUNDERS

That's Field Hudnall on the right, with the ear-to-ear grin. Think the boy likes snow goose hunting in Missouri? PHOTO BY FIELD HUDNALL

and cries are deadly on these birds. With cacklers, I like my B.C. Minima. The pitch is higher still; the secret is rapid, steady clucks.

RANDY BARTZ

You say "Flagman," and the goose hunter you're talking to is going to say Randy Bartz, guaranteed—that's just the way it is. Bartz, who doesn't look 66 and I hope I'm not putting an undeserved year on him, started the flagging craze way back when, and has over the years elevated the simple act of waving a black rag-on-a-stick to an art form. Today, everyone's got one in the blind . . . a Flagman (www.flagmanproducts.com) flag, that is. It's as vital a piece of equipment as are decoys, guns, and bullets.

Bartz on flagging . . . the right way: Instead of waving the flag around in a Figure-8 pattern, you learn to jig it and make it look like a wingbeat. That's the way they were designed. You should try to wrist-jig the flag instead of waving the thing around like a golf club or a baseball bat.

When to stop? Let's say you put the flag down when the birds are 60–70 yards away and go for your gun. You've got them looking at those wings and that's their (landing) target, and then all of a sudden, you quit. It's kind of the same as calling. People say that

The Flagman, Mister Randy Bartz, presents a seminar at the annual Game Fair held near Anoka, Minnesota. A true gentleman, Bartz just flat knows geese.

you don't stop calling at 70 yards 'cause the birds think something's wrong. Well, the same thing applies many times when you're flagging. I think there are a lot of people who aren't taking full advantage of the flags by quitting too soon.

GEORGE LYNCH

Michigan's George Lynch is the blue-collar man's goose hunter—as nice as they come, and as knowledgeable about gunning pressured Canadas as anyone walking. He's a quiet man, save for when he's talking about his favorite subject—geese—or when he's discussing the attributes of his custom call line, interestingly named Lynch Mob Calls.

Lynch on achieving ultimate realism: Successful goose hunting means creating the *illusion* of real geese. Too many hunters just throw decoys randomly with

The man from Michigan, George Lynch. Here, Lynch traveled to Iowa to find this Canada, who was not happy Lynch made the trip. PHOTO BY AVERY PRO-STAFF

Above: Missouri's John Vaca, national sales manager for FA Brands, is at much at home in the duck marsh as he is flat on his back in an Eliminator. PHOTO BY JOHN VACA
Right: This is what the Gurus teach us—how to sucker big Canadas into dropping their inhibitions and doing what we want them to do. PHOTO BY JOE FLADELAND

no plan, and then rely on calling to seal the deal. Not good! You should always open a realistic path to guide the birds where you want them.

I prefer to put my largest decoys, my motion decoys, and my feeders behind the blinds and behind the shooting hole. I'll use GHG's Looker decoys, along with their motion stakes on my feeders, to achieve what I want here. Lesser (smaller) decoys go in front and the sides of the blinds. I truly believe the

larger decoys, coupled with the motion, take the birds' attention away from the blinds (me), while the smaller, lesser decoys in front give the illusion that approaching birds can get closer.

JOHN VACA
Now 41, Missouri's John Vaca began hunting at age 18, and guiding waterfowlers professionally three short years later. His competitive calling career began in

1998, with wins that include the Kansas Grand Slam Open, Rocky Mountain Team Championship, and the '06 North Star Team Champion. He currently serves as the western national sales manager and pro-staff director for FA Brands.

Vaca on staying out of the "Rut": Don't get stuck in a rut and do the same thing every time you go out. You can't be afraid to try something new. A lot of hunters these days pull out the same decoys and put them in the same pattern in the same field all season long. And then they wonder why their only good shooting was the first day or two of the season.

To this end, scouting means more than just finding a field with geese. What are the geese telling you? Are they in one big flock? Family groups? Spread out? Then you need to take what you're told, and transpose that onto your own decoy spread, your blind placement, and your calling.

CHAPTER 14

Specialized Spreads for Canadas

I'M NOT ASHAMED TO SAY IT—I WAS STUMPED. Oh, there were plenty of local birds, and those numbers seemed to be swelling on a daily basis, thanks to strong northwest winds and what appeared to be every Richardson's goose on the planet. The problem wasn't too few birds; oh, no. The problem was doing anything at all with the birds that I had. I'd tried it all: different blind positions, different decoys, different numbers of decoys, down-winding myself. A million combinations, and nothing seemed to work.

After one particularly frustrating evening, I told my wife and gunning partner, Julie, "That's it, I'm calling Freddie Zink." An Ohio boy like myself, Zink had called and worked and carved his way up the ladder until today, he stands at the pinnacle of the goose hunting industry. "Zink will know what to do," I continued. "And if he doesn't . . . hell, I'll go back to squirrel hunting."

So I called Zink and, oddly enough for a day in November, caught him at home. "Take a half dozen feeders," Freddie told me after I'd described my dilemma, "and put 'em in a group. Take four or five walkers, then, and make two downwind legs. Make it as if those birds had just landed, and were walking into

The Guru, Fred Zink, begins to build a Canada spread in Saskatchewan. Watching Zink set decoys compares to watching the late Ansel Adams create his black-and-white photography.

the feeders." I asked about blind placement. The goal, Zink explained, was to shoot left-to-right or right-to-left, and *not* from directly upwind of the feeders. I wasn't going to be shooting the birds in my face, as it were, but rather at an angle; however—and this was the selling point—the birds weren't going to be looking at the blinds on the approach. And it was the blinds, Zink suggested, that were my problem; that, and perhaps the number of decoys I was using, which at the time was 40 to 48 full-bodies. With that, Freddie told me to tell Julie hello, and was gone.

Let me make a long story short. The next evening, on a field I'd hunted with minimal success over the past two weeks, Julie, myself, and our hunting partner, Dave, killed a three-gun limit of six big Canadas. Not over 48 decoys, or 38, or even 18, but over 10: six feeders, and four walkers, two on each side approaching the rest. When they slid in from the north and at a 45-degree angle to the blinds, the birds never knew what hit 'em.

Does it always work that way? Of course not. Can you always expect Freddie Zink to be home in November during goose season? Again, of course not.

My point here is this: There are traditional goose spreads, and then there are twists on the old standards. These aren't necessarily your pull-out-all-the-stops sort of spread; no, sir, they're just a bit different. And that, as call-maker George Lynch of Lynch Mob Calls says, is the key to consistency in goose hunting: "You gotta give 'em something different than everyone else is giving 'em." These, then, are just a little bit different.

DECOY CARE, MAINTENANCE, AND UPGRADING

You can put out the finest goose spread conceivable in terms of numbers, ratio of feeders to resters to sentries, individual decoy placement, and on and on and on, but it's not going to mean a darn thing if the decoys themselves don't look natural. You're just not going to compete in today's tough goose racket if you're not willing to put forth the extra effort.

So number one is to get those decoys clean. According to Zink, it's best to use plain hot water and a stiff-bristled brush to keep your goose decoys looking good. No soap of any kind, Zink cautions, as soap

Loosely spaced but very realistic fully flocked decoys were the keys to success on this Aleutian Canada goose hunt in northern California.

*Sure, it might seem excessive, but these little orange bags keep the decoys
looking as they should—and realistic, natural decoys kill geese.*

Flocked decoys are all the rage right now, and with good reason. They simply look like real geese. PHOTO BY AVERY PRO-STAFF

has the potential to enhance the ultraviolet reflecting properties inherent in the plastics used to make modern decoys. Didn't think of that one, did you? Regardless, keeping them clean is important; no one likes a dirty goose. Dirty geese don't look natural, and a honker that's been up and down the flyway a dozen times knows that.

Secondly, once your decoys are clean, keep them clean. While on a trip with Zink and crew in Saskatchewan last year, I was amazed to see that the boys kept every one of over 200 full-bodied Canada decoys in its own individual drawstring bag. The decoy was taken out of the bag in the morning, hunted over, and returned, if acceptably clean, to the bag at the end of the hunt. If the block had gotten a bit muddy, a small brush was used to remove the dirt before the decoy went into the bag. Type A and anal retentive, you say? Maybe for some, but not for Zink and his outfit who, by the way, are some of the most consistently successful goose hunters in the country. Why?

Because they're Type A and anal retentive when it comes to their decoys, that's why.

Do you have to separately bag each of your decoys in order to achieve success? It can't hurt, but it's not 100 percent necessary. It's simply a matter of taking care of them in transit, in the field, and in storage. When you're setting silhouettes, don't set the stack down in the mud; instead, lay them on a decoy bag, or better, a burlap bag or square of burlap that you carry into the field for just such a purpose. It's elemental not to stack muddy shell on muddy shell on muddy shell, and expect them to be clean. Take a minute as you're setting up or picking up to keep your blocks clean and natural looking, and it'll pay off in birds in the freezer.

And finally, upgrades. Today, a vast majority of the full-bodied Canada goose decoys on the market come standard either with flocked heads and necks, or in many cases, fully flocked bodies. (Flocking is when velvety fibers are glued to portions of the decoy to create a soft, three-dimensional, and thus totally natural appearance.) These are the Cadillacs of goose decoys; however, they're not without their drawbacks, price being one, and care or maintenance being the other. Can't afford flocked or fully flocked decoys? Not to worry, as commercial flocking kits are available, affordable, and easy to use. A few synthetic fibers, a little glue, and a little paint here and there, and you'll have a spread fit for even the most jaded Canada. And what's more, these touch-ups or upgrades can be applied to full-bodies on down to and including silhouettes, so there's no reason today for your spread to look shabby, even if you don't have deep pockets. Remember, decoys work 100 percent on appearance.

SPREADS THROUGH THE SEASON

Now, with your decoys clean, kept clean, and upgraded to the best of your ability and your budget, what do you do with them? First, realize that there is no magic spread that's going to work all the time. There's no number, there's no arrangement, there's no combination of this and that; even the best in the business will tell you that setting a spread for Canadas is guesswork

at best. Certainly, it can be an educated guess taking in consideration your scouting (you did scout, didn't you?), the hunting pressure, the wind direction, the weather, and the number of birds in the area, to name but a few variables; still, it's an educated guess. That said, let's take a look at several Canada goose spreads throughout the season—early, mid-, and late—and how you might apply these modifications, or variations thereof, to your individual hunting situations.

Early Season

Here, let's define the early season as any Canada goose season held in the Lower 48 during the month of September, and perhaps extending into early October; that is, pre- or very, very early migration. In the Canadian provinces, this early portion of the season might be considered the first couple weeks of September—it really depends on how far north your hunt's being conducted. Still, you get the idea.

The junkyard spread: Scott Threinen, a young competitive goose caller from Minnesota and Avery Outdoors pro-staffer, used the term "junkyard spread" in

Attention to details. Here, I'm putting stubble over the black circular bases of these Greenhead Gear fully flocked "Active" (walker) decoys. Personally, I think it makes a huge difference.

The four big Canadas, plus one band (!), in my right hand makes all the struggling and weight worthwhile. This was a late September hunt in Iowa that worked well.

Threinen during the early season (September). Come November, the survivors won't be nearly as easy. PHOTO BY SCOTT THREINEN

*The first of my typical eight to ten "walkers" comes out of Grandpa's pickup
as I ready an afternoon spread in eastern Iowa.*

an interview I did with him a couple years back, and
I just had to ask. As Scott explained it, early season
geese don't have their diplomas yet; that is, they haven't
been subjected to 60 days of hunting pressure, thus
they're not as wary as they might be come November.
As such, these naïve birds can often be duped with a
combination spread of silhouettes, shells, full-bodies,
or whatever a hunter has available. Dirty, clean, lop-
sided—it really doesn't matter. The key, says Threinen,
is to progress with your decoy spread as the birds
themselves progress, or grow wiser. And—this is
important—not to show your entire hand the first
week of the season. "Don't hand these birds their
diplomas," says Threinen. "Make 'em earn it." There's
no need to come out of the starting gate with ten
dozen fully flocked full-bodies; keep those in reserve
until you really need them. And you will, trust me.

A family affair: Small family groups of widely
spaced Canada decoys—five here, four there, another
four over there—are an excellent idea during the early
season when the birds themselves are in family groups.
It's a natural grouping for Canadas at this time of year,
and that's what you want to present. Realize, though,
that family groups don't necessarily carry on through-

out the season. Once the weather turns and food
sources go from aplenty to a premium, it's every bird
for himself; thus, you're either dealing with the Big
Black Blob Theory of goose decoy placement—especially true with the smaller subspecies like lessers or
cacklers—or individual decoys placed more or less an
equal distance apart. Here, the lesson is the more you
know and understand about Canada goose biology, the
better equipped you are to set a realistic spread.

Mid-Season

Walking 'em in: I hate to repeat myself, but I'm going
to in this case simply because Zink's tactic of walking
them in not only worked well in the opening segment,
but has continued to produce consistently over the past
couple seasons. Geese are greedy, gregarious birds—
always hungry, and always eager to jump into the middle of what might be a free meal. And Zink's walking
goose spread plays on that biological characteristic.
This specialty spread works well, too, I believe, due
to other variables. One, a 10- or 12-decoy spread isn't
what most mid-season Canadas are accustomed to
seeing, so it's different, and that's a good thing. Two,
with the blinds off to one side as opposed to the tradi-

tional directly upwind *and* if you practice good movement discipline—that is, don't move until it's time to shoot—the birds will never know you're there.

Late season

Shells on snow or frozen ground: "I do most of my late season hunting in northern Nevada or Colorado," said Chad Belding, competitive goose caller and Avery

Outdoors pro-staffer, "where frozen ground, heavy frost, or snow is a common thing. I use almost exclusively shells at this time because often the first thing Canadas do when they hit these hard fields is lay down. There may be a couple standing guard, but almost all of the birds will be laying down. They're letting their body heat melt the snow or frost or ground enough so they can get to the food

Left: An ultra-realistic mixed late-season spread. Note the "lunch lines" walking into the main body of the rig. PHOTO BY JOE FLADELAND *Above: Shells—or full-bodies with the legs removed—used on snow or ice can be incredibly effective during the late season; still, not too many 'fowlers, relatively speaking, take advantage of this technique.* PHOTO BY AVERY PRO-STAFF

underneath. Then they'll simply eat where they're at— just peck at the ground without getting up."

Before commercial sleeper decoys were available, Belding used shells minus the heads in order to present that "all tucked in" look. Today, though, he doesn't find it necessary to go headless. "I like the Greenhead Gear oversized shells with the flocked heads," he said. "They're very realistic, and are the exact body posture

of a Canada lying on the ground." Fully flocked decoys, he claims, are even better on snow or ice or under extremely cold conditions. "The flocking— those tiny poly-fibers—retain heat better and longer, and help the decoy resist frosting."

CHAPTER 15

Today's Hunter:
The Modern PR Specialist

IT WAS THE LATE 1980S. MICK JAGGER HADN'T yet reached retirement age, and I was working in a public information capacity for the Ohio Department of Natural Resources (ODNR) Division of Wildlife in Columbus. My job at the time was assisting in the coordination of all the hunter education courses across the state, so when the lady called asking about muskrats—well, the truth was, she had the wrong number. Or at least the wrong department.

"I'd like to find a trapper." The female voice at the other end of the line carried a definite air of frustration. "Well, ma'am," I told her, "you've reached the Outdoor Skills Unit, and we address hunter education questions . . . but, maybe there's something that I can help you with."

The problem, it turned out, was muskrats. It seems the lady and her husband had moved out of the city and had built themselves quite a nice country home, complete with a two-acre pond. The two of them, she continued, had decided to accentuate the pond with rather expensive water lilies and other plants—all of which the friendly neighborhood muskrats immediately devoured. Undaunted, she and her husband replanted; however, they soon discovered that their money was funding little more than a nightly aquatic

Wood ducks, Canadas, whitetails, turkeys, muskrats—it doesn't matter the quarry. We're all hunters and consumptive users, and as such, it's imperative we're united. PHOTO BY JOE FLADELAND

buffet for what she was certain were hoards of bother-some rodents.

"I'm running a short trapline now," I told the lady, her story done. "And if you're interested, I'd be more than happy to come out and take care of the problem personally." With that, she brightened noticeably, and was anything but slow in providing me their address and detailed directions.

That next Saturday, I made the half-hour drive beyond the Columbus city limits to the folks' place on the Southside. Sure enough, they had a pretty little pond, and sure enough, they had a muskrat problem. After a quick walk-around, I sat with the homeowners and gave them my suggestions, which, in a nutshell, had me running a small trapline and, hopefully, rid-ding them of their dilemma. "But we have dogs," the lady-of-the-house said, concern in her voice. "And then there's the grandkids. And us. Isn't there a dan-ger?" They were legitimate questions; fortunately, I had an answer prepared. With the owners at my side,

I demonstrated a #110 conibear and explained how I planned to use only these types of traps. More impor-tantly, the entire line would be submerged so as to eliminate non-target catches, the owners included. I then took the pair outside and asked them to watch as I made my first set at the mouth of an active muskrat den, explaining what I was doing and why. Each thanked me for putting them at ease and went indoors, while I made a trip round the pond setting more than two dozen #110s in active dens and underwater runs.

At this juncture, let me make a long story short. Although, much to the homeowners' delight, I caught 30 or so 'rats out of the little pond, I had to explain the fact that because the pond had creeks flowing both in and out, they would in all likelihood see a steady pro-cession of critters munching on their water plants; however, I assured them that all they had to do was call, and I'd come out and run another string. "Do you ever hunt pheasants?" the lady-of-the-house asked as I shook her hand and started toward my truck.

Take the time to tell non-hunters about your chosen activities. Answer their questions; show them your photographs. The mind you change may make a difference at the ballot box one day.

*Left: Realize that, yes, we hunters are predators, but our outdoor pursuits aren't solely about the kill. **Above:** Many wild populations—pintails, for instance—benefit greatly from the efforts of hunters, and it's very important that we let the American public know this fact.* PHOTO BY JOE FLADELAND

"I do," I said, trying—I think unsuccessfully—to hide a growing smile. "My husband and I have never let anyone hunt out back, but you're welcome to. And there's plenty of pheasants around. Just be careful, and let us know when you're coming out . . . and thanks again," she finished and turned back inside. By the time I hit the 270 Bypass on the edge of town, my face hurt from grinning.

An interesting story, yes, but what's the point? Today, more than ever, consumptive users of our natural resources—that is, we hunters and trappers—need to be public relations (PR) specialists first, and consumptive users second. Without the first, the second often is non-existent. And this PR aspect as it relates to the consumptive sports, now in the twenty-first century, goes far beyond an individual's ability to ask for and obtain permission to use privately owned land. True, the art of gaining access to private lands for the purpose of hunting or trapping—or any type of activity for that matter—is indeed just that, an art; however, with consumptive users under intense scrutiny and, often and unfortunately, under a constant barrage of negative criticism by an uninformed general public, the ability to present ourselves and our outdoor pursuits in a favorable light is

more important—and at times, more difficult—than ever before.

Many hunters and trappers will agree on what constitutes bad or negative public relations. Hunting out of season, shooting multiple limits of game, trespassing—they're all recognized as examples of what *not* to do. That said, there are many differing opinions on how hunters and trappers might go about presenting themselves in a favorable light—or rather, perpetuating this idea of the consumptive user as a PR specialist.

In my way of thinking, today's hunter and trapper deals or comes into contact with three diverse groups of people. And it's how he or she interacts with these individual groups that forms the foundation of the modern consumptive user as a PR specialist. These collectives are:

THE HUNTER/TRAPPER

Time and again we hunters and trappers hear the phrase "We're our own worst enemy," meaning that we as consumptive users, although having the ability and the opportunity to paint a positive picture, choose not to for one reason or another, particularly, and that's the key word here, in our dealings with other consumptive users and user groups. Simply put, hunters and trap-

*Black Lab. Yellow Lab. Chesapeake Bay Retriever. We're dog men,
as we are hunters, and we must present ourselves as such.*

pers often have a difficult, if not impossible, time playing well together, and it's not unusual for these differences of opinion to be very publicly and very passionately displayed. And that's not a good thing.

True, hunters and trappers aren't going to agree on all fronts; to hope for such is unrealistic. Individual A supports trapping, while Individual B doesn't. Bait and hounds are fine for one, and not so for another. To disagree is not the problem; however, to present anything less than a united front to the masses serves to do nothing but chip away at the foundation of hunting and trapping as a whole.

If there is indeed a bottom line in the case of hunters dealing with hunters as that interaction relates to the conveyance of positive public relations to the general public, it's the elimination of dissention among the ranks of the consumptive user. We are hunters; we are trappers, and it's vital that we present that united front. To fight among ourselves is without question the worst of all possible PR situations.

THE NON-HUNTER/TRAPPER

First, let me make the distinction between non-hunters and anti-hunters. Non-hunters have no strong feelings one way or another toward the consumptive sports. These people are uninformed; they straddle the proverbial fence. However, they are also members of the voting public, and poor PR on the part of the consumptive user can push them into to next category, the anti-hunter, where their ballot against a dove bill or a trapping initiative can have a tremendous impact on the opportunities that we consumptive users currently enjoy.

In the case of non-hunters or trappers, public relations and education should be considered synonymous

terms. Take, for instance, the trapping example above. These particular landowners, despite their problem, were tentative about accepting my proposed remedy. Why? They knew nothing about trapping, and the role of the trapper as wildlife manager. In this case, the time spent educating these individuals paid dividends that reached far beyond the handful of pelts I stretched or the roosters I took home. Simply put, these folks now looked at the consumptive of our natural resources in a different—that is, more positive—light, and as newly educated individuals, would hopefully carry that education through in their dealings with other non-hunters.

Left: Take a minute, and think before you speak as hunter. Choose your words carefully, and be prepared to answer questions. Below: Public events such as this program held at Mack's Prairie Wings in Stuttgart, Arkansas, provide an excellent opportunity to present our *side of the story.*
PHOTO BY AVERY PRO-STAFF

Facing page: The Golden Age of Waterfowling is today. Let's not let it fade into the sunset. PHOTO BY AVERY PRO-STAFF

Boys and girls such as this young hunter are truly the future of hunting in North America. Are you giving them every opportunity you possibly can?

THE ANTI-HUNTER/TRAPPER

It is possible to encounter an anti-hunter who will indeed listen to the consumptive use side of the natural resources story. I would consider such a meeting uncommon; however, it does happen. My wife, Julie, and I currently hunt whitetails on a small property near Cedar Rapids, Iowa, owned by a former female member of the anti-hunting faction. Upon moving out of the city proper and into the "country," this particular lady found herself set upon by hoards of hungry deer—roses, petunias, peonies, shrubs, apple trees . . . nothing was safe. When her first attempts at dissuading the voracious herds failed, she sought guidance from the director of a local nature preserve—a gentleman with years of outdoor education who, fortunately for us, just so happened to be a blackpowder enthusiast. One thing lead to another, introductions were made, and today, the lady welcomes us each fall with open arms.

On the other side, there are anti-hunters for whom an open mind is a concept unimaginable. These individuals have set their course and will not waver. So what does the consumptive user/PR specialist do in such a case? Intelligent, educated, and rational discussion (note: I didn't say heated argument) on the hunter or trapper's part is always an option; however, presented with a boisterous audience unwilling to listen to a second side of the story, there's absolutely nothing wrong nor cowardly with discontinuing the conversation altogether. In such a case, it's often best to save your breath and save your communicative strength in favor of a more likely victory.

Interacting—and interacting well—with the general public on issues concerning the consumptive use of our natural resources, i.e. hunting and trapping, can present a challenge; however, armed with education, patience, and a willingness to listen and discuss wisely, the transformation from hunter or trapper to public relations specialist can be easily and effectively achieved. It's a responsibility and a role we all must assume from time to time, and done correctly and efficiently, will help carry the consumptive sports throughout the twenty-first century and beyond.

Manufacturers' Listing

Aero Outdoors
316 East "B" Circle
Pasco, WA 99301
509-545-8000
www.aerooutdoors.com

Alex Langbell—Craig Riche—Steve Schulz
Columbia Basin Waterfowl
4302 Polo Way
West Richland, WA 99353
509-728-0145
www.basinwaterfowl.com

Allen-Curtis Waterfowl Adventures
Christian Curtis & Keith Allen
508 W. Salcedo
Sikeston, MO 63801
573-380-0032
www.wildfowladventures.com

Arborwear
PO Box 341
Chagrin Falls, OH 44022
1-888-578-TREE
www.arborwear.com

Avery Outdoors
PO Box 820176
Memphis, TN 38112
901-324-1500
www.averyoutdoors.com

Ballistic Specialties
PO Box 2401
Batesville, AR 72503
800-276-2550
www.angleport.com

Bass Pro Shops
2500 E. Kearney
Springfield, MO 65898
www.basspro.com

Benelli USA
17603 Indian Head Hwy.
Accokeek, MD 20607
www.benelliusa.com

Bill Blakeley
Blue Bank Resort/Reelfoot Lake
3330 State Route 21 E
Tiptonville, TN 38079
877-BLUEBANK
www.bluebankresort.com

Bill Saunders Guide Series Calls
1008 W. 37th Place
Kennewick, WA 99337
509-582-0190
www.guideseriescalls.com

Birchwood Casey
7900 Fuller Rd.
Eden Prairie, MN 55344
www.birchwoodcasy.com

Blue Bank Resort—Classic gunning
    on Reelfoot Lake
813 Lake Dr.
Hornbeak, TN 38232
877-258-3226
www.bluebankresort.com

Browning
One Browning Place
Morgan, UT 84050
www.browning.com

Buck Gardner Calls
2129 Troyer Ave., Bldg. 249, Ste. 104
Memphis, TN 38114
www.buckgardner.com

Bushnell Sports Optics
9200 Cody
Overland Park, KS 66214
www.bushnell.com

Cabela's
One Cabela's Drive
Sidney, NE 69160
www.cabelas.com

Carry-Lite Decoys
3601 Jenny Lind Rd.
Fort Smith, AR 72902
www.carrylitedecoys.com

Carstens Industries, Inc.
PO Box 185
Melrose, MN 56352
www.carstensindustries.com

Coyote Company Leather
3706 Yaupon Dr.
Grand Prairie, TX 75052
www.coyotecoleather.com

DeLorme Mapping
Two Delorme Dr.
Yarmouth, ME 04096
www.delorme.com

Drake Waterfowl
910 E. Goodman Rd., Suite F
Southaven, MS 38671
662-349-9398
www.drakewaterfowl.com

Enviro-Metal, Inc.
1307 Clark Mill Rd.
Sweet Home, OR 97386
www.hevishot.com

Federal Cartridge Company
    (Blount, Inc.)
900 Ehlen Dr.
Anoka, MN 55303
www.federalcartridge.com

Final Approach Blinds
205 N. Depot St.
Fox Lake, WI 53933
877-956-5746
www.finalapproachblinds.com

Fisher Beavertail
211 Northwest 1st St.
Avon, MN 56310
www.fisherbeavertail.com

Foiles Migrators, Inc.
800 W. Quincy St., Box 457
Pleasant Hill, IL 62366
217-734-1434
www.foilesstraitmeat.com

George Lynch
Lynch Mob Calls
9032 Bay Creek Rd.
Erie, MI 48113
734-915-9487
www.lynchmobcallsinc.com

Gerber Legendary Blades
14200 SW 72nd Ave.
Portland, OR 97223
www.gerberblades.com

Hard Core Decoys
214 E. 34th St.
Garden City, ID 83714
www.hardcoredecoys.com

Haydel's Game Calls
5018 Hazel Jones Rd.
Bossier City, LA 71111
318-746-3586
www.haydels.com

Hunter's Specialties
6000 Huntington Ct. NE
Cedar Rapids, IA 52402
www.hunterspec.com

Kent Cartridge America, Inc.
PO Box 849
Kearneysville, WV 25430
www.kentgamebore.com

Knight & Hale Game Calls
Drawer 670
Cadiz, KY 42211
www.knight-hale.com

Mighty Layout Boys
1215 State St.
Hobart, IN 46342
www.mightylayoutboys.com

MOJO Decoys
PO Box 1640
Bastrop, LA 71221
www.MojoMallard.com

MoMarsh
21 White River Lane
Defiance, MO 63341
www.momarsh.com

Mossy Oak Clothing—Haas Outdoors
PO Box 757
West Point, MS 39773
www.mossyoak.com

Quaker Boy Game Calls
5455 Webster Rd.
Orchard Park, NY 14127
www.quakerboygamecalls.com

Randy Bartz & Flagman Products
Box 301
Oronoco, MN 55960
800-575-4782
www.flagmanproducts.com

Remington Arms Company
870 Remington Dr.
Madison, NC 27025
www.remington.com

Rich-N-Tone (RNT)
PO Box 1026
Stuttgart, AR 72160
www.rntcalls.com

Rocky Shoes & Boots, Inc.
39 Canal St.
Nelsonville, OH 45764
www.rockyboots.com

Tanglefree
PO Box 1280
Clayton, CA 94517
www.tanglefree.com

Tim Grounds
Tim Grounds Championship Calls
1414 Barham St.
Johnston City, IL 62951
618-983-5649
www.timgrounds.com

Vito A. Angelone
Widgeon Bay Watermen
1200 N. Timber Ridge Rd.
Cross Junction, VA 22625
www.widgeonbaywatermen.com

Winchester
427 N. Shamrock St.
East Alton, IL 49685
www.winchester.com

Zink Calls
9132 Barnes Rd.
Clayton, OH 45315
www.zinkcalls.com

Index

Page numbers in italics indicate
   illustrations.
Page numbers in bold indicate
   sidebars.

advancement, xiii–xv
aerial photography website, **81**
Akin, Tommy, *79*
ammunition
   for goose hunting, 94, *96*
   Hevi-Shot, 111
   non-steel non-toxic, 99
   for rail hunting, 111
   for snipe hunting, 116
   Winchester light 12 load, 111
   Winchester light steel loads, 111
AquaPod boats, *12–13*, 42, *44*, *47*,
   48, *52*
Ash, Gil, 84, 132–33, *133*, *140*
   on shooting school, 134–39
Ash, Vicki, 84, 132–33
Avery Outdoors, 144, 171
   Finisher blind bags, 70, 74
   Floating blind bags, 66
   Floating Pit Bags, 75
   Power Hunter blind bags, 71
   Pro-Grade blind bags, 73
   website, **80**

Bartz, Randy, 96, *149*
   on goose hunting, 149
Beaver Dam Hunting Services, 75
Belding, Chad, 59, *61*, 64–67, *66*, *145*
   duck call experience, 61–62
   on goose hunting, 144–45
   on using shells, 160–61
Beyer, Paul, *57*
Bires, Greg, 32

Bismuth Cartridge Company, 111
blind bags, 64, *74*
   Avery Floating, 66
   Avery Outdoors Finisher, 70, 74
   Avery Outdoors Floating Pit, 75
   Avery Power Hunter, 71
   Avery Pro-Grade, 73
   Drake Waterfowl Systems Floating, 69
   FA Gunner, 68
   Final Approach All-Season, 68
   well-stocked, *65*, 85, *86*
blinds
   for diver hunting, 10
   for goose hunting, 94, *96*, 98
   for layout hunting, 46
   low-profile, 99
   for snow goose hunting, *126*
boats, 42–47, *43*, 89–90
   AquaPod, *12–13*, 42, *44*, *47*
   Carstens Canvasback, *46–47*
   diver hunting, 10
   layout, 39, 48–51, **52**
   marsh, 48, **52**
   scull, 51–53, **52**
   sneakboats, 46–48, **52**
   TDB, *20*
Bourjaily, Phil, 42, 114, *117*, *140*
   rail hunting, *113*
   on shooting school, 139–40
Boyd, Lamar, 75, *75*
Boyd, Mike, 75
Browning, 171
   Citori Lightning Feather 20-gauge
     gun, 109, *109*
Buckingham, Nash, 75
Buckley, Bill, *63*

Calamus Resevoir, Nebraska, diver
   hunting in, **15**

Calef, Barnie, 36
   duck call experience, 63
calls, duck and goose, 54–56, *55*, *88*,
   94–96, *96*, *101*, 146, 147
   Hess's, *56*
   horror stories concerning, 60–63
   Kelley Powers Triple Crown, 69
   learning about, 88–89
   OLT A-50, 99
   OLT D-2, 54
   reeds, 99, *99*
   Rich-n-Tone, 69
   routine care of, 59
   SR-1 Paralyzer, *60*
   storage of, 60
   trimming reeds of, *59*
   troubleshooting guide for, 57–58
   tuning, 58–59, 100
   volume, 100
   wood, *56*
   Zink, 69
camouflage and concealment, 85, *85*,
   89, 91
Carlson, Wendell, 36
Carsten Industries, Inc., 171
   Canvasback boats, *46–47*, 48
Cassidy, Sam, 22
Chesapeake Bay, diver hunting in, **15**
Columbia Basin Waterfowl, 73, 171
Columbia River, diver hunting in, **15**
Cooksey, Bill, 58, *58*, *59*, 60

Davis, Andy, *53*
decoys, *91*
   canvasback, *x*, *1*, *35*
   care of, 154–55
   for diver hunting, 11–13
   flocked, *156*, 156–57, *157*
   goldeneye, *18*

for goose hunting, 96, 149–50
hand-carved, *33, 87,* 88
harlequin, *26*
for layout hunting, 39
maintenance of, *155,* 156, *156*
oldsquaw, *24, 25*
scoter, *22, 23*
sleeping, *84*
snow geese, *102, 103, 123, 124, 125*
swimming, 89
upgrading, 90, 156–57
wood duck, *163*
see also spreads
Delta Waterfowl website, **80**
Devil's Lake, North Dakota, diver
    hunting in, **15**
diver hunting, 5, 7–10
    blinds, 10
    boats, 10
    decoy and line organization, *14*
    decoys, 11–13
    guns for, 14
    increased popularity in, 4–7
    on Mississippi River, *6*
    traditional waters for, **15**
dogs, **49,** *166*
    Jet, *2, 105, 112, 116*
    Maggie, *111, 116*
    Ruff, *xiii, 126*
Drake Waterfowl, 172
    Systems Floating Blind Bags, 69
duck calls, *see* calls, duck and goose
Duck Hunters' Boat Page website, **52**
Duck Hunter's Refuge website, **80**
Duck Hunting Chat website, **80**
ducks, *32*
    bufflehead, 8
    canvasback, 7
    diver, 7–10
    drake, *3*
    eider, *19,* 19–22
    goldeneye, 8–9, *10*
    harlequin, 17, 25–28, **26–27**
    merganser, 9–10
    oldsquaw, 24
    pintail, *165*
    preparing and cooking, 14
    redhead, 8, *9*
    ringneck, 9, *10*
    scaup (bluebills), *7,* 8, *9, 35, 40*
    scoter, 22–23, *23*
    surf scoter, *17*
Ducks Unlimited website, **80**
Dzedo Johnson Shooting School, 130

FA Gunner blind bags, 68
Fat Boys boats, 48
Field & Stream, 139
Final Approach Blinds, 146, 172
    All-Season blind bags, 68

Fish & Wildlife Service website, **81**
fish and wildlife websites, state, **80**
flagging, *97*
    divers, *34*
    geese, 96, *125,* 149
flocking, 156–57
Franklin, Mike, *148*

geese, *101*
    Canada, *84, 88, 95, 97, 143,*
        150–51
    snow, *119*
    understanding, 100
Google Earth website, **81**
goose calls, *see* calls, duck and goose
goose hunting, 94, 142–51
    ammunition for, 94, *96,* 99
    asking questions concerning, 99
    Bartz on, 149
    being invisible while, 96
    Belding on, 144–45
    blinds, 94, *96, 98*
    calls and calling, 94–96, *96,* 99, *99,*
        100, *101,* 146, 147–49
    decoys, 96, 149–50
    early season, 96
    flagging, 96, *97,* 149
    freelance, 144
    Grounds on, 146
    Hudnall on, 147
    late-season, 147
    Latschaw on, 146–47
    location, 102
    low-profile blinds, 99
    Lynch on, 149–50
    motion, 99
    patterning, 99
    Saunders on, 147–49
    scouting, 99, *100–1,* 145
    spreads, 96, 152–61
    Stahl on, 145
    staying out of the rut when, 151
    Threinen on, 145–46
    understanding geese, 100
    Vaca on, 150–51
    versatility, 146
    wind direction, 102
    year-round, 103
    Zink on, 142–44
    see also snow goose hunting
Goose Pit Kennels, 67
Grounds, Hunter, 146
Grounds, Tim, 64, 89, 96, *146*
    on goose hunting, 146
guns
    Browning Citori Lightning Feather
        20-gauge, 109, *109*
    fit, 137
    Model 24 16-gauge, *139*
    for rail hunting, 109–11

Remington 870 Youth Model
    20-gauge, 109
Remington M11-87 12-gauge, *110*
for snipe hunting, 116
Winchester Super X2, 14
Winchester Super X3, *14*

Harstad, Lee, *15*
Hess, Doug, 54–56, 60
    calls troubleshooting guide by, 57–58
    on tuning calls, 58–59
Hevi-Shot shotshells, 111
Hiney boats, 51
Hoot ETV, *53*
Howard, Kevin, *8*
    with Winchester Super X3, *14*
Hudnall, Field, *63,* 69–71, *70,* 89, *96, 148*
    duck call experience, 62
    on goose hunting, 147
Humboldt boats, 51

The Impoundments, diver hunting in, **15**
Internet scouting, 76–81
    comaraderie in, 80–81
    convenience of, 79–80
    current information available by, 79
    websites, **80–81**

Jackson, Todd, *21,* 21–22
Jim Johnson School, 130
John Redmond Resevoir, Kansas, diver
    hunting in, **15**
Johnson, Julia, *34, 35,* 42
Johnson, M. D.
    on Columbia River, *9*
    on combination rail/snipe hunt, *116*
    diving ducks on Columbia River, *xv, 2*
    dropping anchors, *12*
    flocking decoys, *157*
    layout hunting, *31, 41*
    rail hunting, *105, 106, 110, 111*
    sea duck hunting, *28, 29*
    setting-up spread, *159*
Johnson, Mick, *117*

Keller, Tyson, 118, *120,* 120–21, *126, 128*
    snow goose hunting strategies by,
        121–29
Kelley Powers Triple Crown goose calls, 69

Langbell, Alex, *72,* 72–73
Latschaw, Ron, *147, 148*
    on goose hunting, 146–47
Lausman, Carl, *70*
layout hunting, xii, *40, 41*
    about, 38–39
    blinds, 46
    decoys, 39
    the Mighty Layout Boys and, 32–36
    on Mississippi River, 36–41

tender boats, 39
traditional, 32
LOWE boats, 51
Lynch, George, on goose hunting, 149–50
Lynch Mob Calls, 154, 172

McCauley, Ian, *51*
McMahan, Jimmy, 68
The Mallard Club website, **80**
manufacturers, listing of, 171–72
Merrymeeting Bay boats, 51
Mick Johnson School of Shotgun
    Shooting, 130
Mighty Layout Boys, 32–36, 172
    boats, 48
Miller, Nick, 42, *79*
Miller, Tony, *4*, 14, 42, *47*
Minchk, Dan, xv, 37, 44
Minchk, Mike, xv, 14, *36*, 44
    layout hunting on Mississippi River,
        36–41, *37, 38*
Mississippi River, diver hunting on, **15**
Model 24 16-gauge gun, *139*
Moutoux, Mike, **107**, 114
Mueller, Travis, *49*

National Weather Service website, **80–81**
Neal Verity School, 130

Optimum Shooting Performance
    school, 133

pass-shooting, 85
patterning, 84, *85*
    goose hunting, 99
Powers, Kelley, *68*, 68–69, 146
public relations, 162–68
    anti-hunters, 168
    events, *167*
    hunters and trappers, 165–66
    non-hunters, 166–67
    obtaining permission to use private
        land, 165
Puddler boats, 48

rail hunting, 104–14, *105, 106, 108, 110,
    111, 113*
    clothing and accessories for, 111–13,
        112
    guns and ammunition for, 109–11
    mentor, **107**
    season, 108–9
rails
    clapper, 107
    cleaning, 114
    cooking, 114
    king, 107–8
    sora, 106–7
    species of, 106
    Virginia, 106

Reder, Tom, 32
Remington Arms Company, 172
    870 Youth Model 20-gauge gun, 109
    M11-87 12-gauge, *110*
Riche, Craig, 73
Rich-n-Tone, 172
    Calls, 69
River Mallard Calls, 56
Robey, Clint, *49*
    pulling lightweight skiff into cattails, *45*
Rongers, John, *50*
Rongers, Mark, *xi, 50*
    foreword by, xi–xii
    on layout hunting, 32–36

satellite imagery website, **81**
Saunders, Bill, *62, 67*, 67–68, *148*
    duck call experience, 62
    on goose hunting, 147–49
scouting, 99, *100–1*, 121, 145
    see also Internet scouting
sculling, *51*, 52–53
Sea Duck Authorization Card, 27
sea duck hunting, 16–19, *21*
    eiders, 19–22
    harlequins, 25–28
    oldsquaws, 24
    scoters, 22–23
Shepard, Mike, 38
    layout hunting on Mississippi River, *37*
shooting
    experience, 138
    instinctive, 134
    moving muzzle with target, 137–38
    proficiency, 135–36
shooting school, 130–40, *135, 136,
    137,* 138
    becoming a better shooter by attending,
        84, 134–35
    clinics, 134
    cost of, 139
    guns used in, 137
    instruction, 138–39
    students, 134
    when should attend, 136
Shultz, Steve, 73
skiffs, *see* boats
Slyfield, Fred, 8–9
Slyfield, Hunter, 8–9
Slyfield, Spencer, 8–9
Smith, Tab, 67
sneakboats, 47–48, **52**
    Barnegat Bay, 47, 48
    Carstens Canvasback, 48
    definition of, 46–47
snipe, *114*
snipe hunting, 114–16, *117*
    guns and ammunition for, 116
    rail hunting combination, *116*
    tale, **115**

snow geese, *129*
snow goose hunting, 118–29, *122, 127,
    128*
    blinds, *126*
    flagging, *125*
    scouting, *121*
    spread, *123*
    strategies, 121–29
spreads
    Canada goose, 152–61, *153, 154*
    combining species in, 86, *87*
    downsizing, 91
    early season, 157, *158*
    goose, 96
    junkyard, 157–59
    late-season, 147, 160–61, *160–61*
    mid-season, 159–60
    mixed, 86, *87*
    upgrading, 90
    walking goose, 159–60
Stahl, Shawn, xv, 96, 99, *145*
    on goose hunting, 145
Stanley, Allan, 89
Stealth boats, 48
strategies, hunting, 82–84
    adding coots, 90
    attention to detail, 89
    back away from blocks, 90
    being mobile, 91
    blind bags, well-stocked, 85, *86*
    boat size, 89–90
    camouflage and concealment, 85, *85,* 91
    combining species in decoy spreads,
        86, *87*
    creating on-the-water motion, 89
    downsizing spreads, 91
    education, 89
    efficiency, 89
    hand-carved decoys, 88
    hunting with experienced hunters, 92
    hunting mid-morning flight, 91–92
    learning calls, 88–89
    location, 85
    long-term waterfowl storage, 92
    moving water, 85
    observation, 89
    pass-shooting, 85
    patterning, 84, *85*
    practice, 93
    realism and natural movement, 85
    shooting lessons, 84
    silhouettes, 86
    sleeping on ice, 84
    snow geese, 121–29
    swimming decoys, 89
    travel, 92
    upgrading decoy spread, 90
    see also individual types of waterfowl
        hunting
Sur-Shot Retrievers, 68

Sutton, Steve, xv, 14, 16–18, *18*, *27*
    sea duck hunting, *28*, *29*

TerraServer website, **81**
Threinen, Scott, 89, 96, *96*, *146*
    duck call experience, 60
    early season goose hunting, *158*
    on goose hunting, 145–46
    on junkyard spread, 157–59
tide tables website, **81**
topographical information website, **81**
TopoZone website, **81**
Toye, Tony, 2

U.S. Geological Survey website, **81**
UFO boats, 48

Vaca, John, *150*
    on goose hunting, 150–51
vacuum packer, *93*
Vandemore, Tony, *49*, *71*, 71–72, 118, 120, *120*, *128*
    snow goose hunting strategies by, 121–29
Vilsack, Tom, 108

Waterfowler.com website, **80**
waterfowling, 77, *83*, *93*, *131*, *132*, *141*, *164*, *165*, *166*, *169*
    in Iowa, *xiv*
    see also individual types of waterfowl hunting

websites, **80–81**
Wilson, Curt, *73*, 73–75
Winchester, 172
    light 12 load shotshells, 111
    light steel loads shotshells, 111
Wolski, Mike, *11*

youth hunters, *168*

Zink, Fred, 64, 69, 89, *102*, 103, *144*, 152, *153*, 156
    on goose hunting, 142–44
    on walking goose spread, 159–60
Zink Calls, 69, 144, 172